Dublin

Text by Alice Fellows
Updated and edited by Jason Mitchell
Principal photographer: Richard Nowitz
Cover photograph by Doug Plummer
Layout Concept: Klaus Geisler
Managing Editor: Tony Halliday

Berlitz® POCKET GUIDE
Dublin

Sixth Edition 2003

Photography by:
Richard Nowitz 1, 6, 11, 22, 24, 29, 30, 31, 33, 34, 35, 40, 42, 43, 44, 45, 48, 58, 72, 80, 88, 93, 94, 99; Doug Plummer 15, 18, 26, 36, 39, 47, 49, 50, 52, 54, 57, 60, 62, 65, 66, 75, 78, 82, 95, 100, 103; Geray Sweeney 8, 16, 25, 46, 69, 71, 85, 86, 90; Marcus Wilson-Smith 77, 87, 96.

CONTACTING THE EDITORS
Every effort has been made to provide accurate information in this publication, but changes are inevitable. The publisher cannot be responsible for any resulting loss, inconvenience or injury. We would appreciate it if readers would call our attention to any errors or outdated information by contacting Berlitz Publishing, PO Box 7910, London SE1 1WE, England. Fax: (44) 20 7403 0290; e-mail: berlitz@apaguide.co.uk www.berlitzpublishing.com

All Rights Reserved

© *2003 Apa Publications GmbH & Co. Verlag KG, Singapore Branch, Singapore Maps © 2003 Apa Publications GmbH & Co. Verlag KG, Singapore Branch, Singapore*

Printed in Singapore by Insight Print Services (Pte) Ltd, 38 Joo Koon Road, Singapore 628990. Tel: (65) 6865-1600. Fax: (65) 6861-6438

Berlitz Trademark Reg. U.S. Patent Office and other countries. Marca Registrada

➤
Temple Bar, a network of narrow streets with some of the best bars in town (page 37)

Dublin Castle, the centre of English rule in Ireland for seven centuries (page 40)

◄

The Guinness Storehouse tour. Learn all about brewing and sample the freshest pint in town (page 45)

▼

TOP TEN ATTRACTIONS

Powerscourt Estate, a Palladian-style mansion set in splendid formal gardens, is an easy day trip from Dublin (page 72)

One of Dublin's most elegant landmarks, the Custom House dominates the north bank of the Liffey (page 59)

St Stephen's Green, a park in the heart of the city flanked by some fine buildings, including the Shopping Centre (page 34)

The Dublin Writers Museum honours the literary greats, from Beckett to Joyce, Shaw and Yeats (page 64)

Kilmainham Gaol. Learn about life behind bars and and what brought prisoners here (page 46)

Christ Church, one of the city's two major cathedrals (page 42)

Trinity College. Dublin's University has a string of famous alumni and owns treasures such as *The Book of Kells* (page 27)

CONTENTS

Fact Sheets

DUBLIN AND THE DUBLINERS

Dublin seems to be changing before your very eyes. New construction is everywhere, traffic is increasingly congested, and the frenetic pace of rush hour couldn't set a more contrasting tone to that of the peaceful countryside. At night the streets are crowded with people bent on having a good time. Though the global economy may be taking a rest, prosperity is still in the air of this young capital and the roar of the 'Celtic Tiger' has yet to quieten.

The proverbial hospitality and warm welcome have not vanished in this new bustle, though the city's character is more complex than the souvenir shops suggest. Dublin sits on 1,000 years of history – and it is present everywhere, from the famous literary homes on Merrion Square to the bullet holes on the General Post Office (the paintings inside give a quick lesson). That history, along with recent prosperity has given birth to a new culture that is now a trendsetter in the arts, design and, of course, music; an exciting development that merits leaving the pub behind for a while and seeing what the new Irish are all about.

Along the cobbled lanes of Temple Bar, rubbing shoulders with dozens of theme bars selling the Ireland of leprechauns and legend, are galleries showing off a new generation of artists and photographers whose talent looks to a world stage. Fashion designers have made haute couture out of hand knits and tweeds. Musicians have proven you don't need a bodhrán to make it in Irish music. Boutiques sell ultra-modern, Irish designed furnishings.

Prosperity has also brought with it a new emphasis on historic preservation. Dublin excels in packaging its past for the

The rotunda and columns of City Hall

The Ha'penny Bridge across the River Liffey

visitor. You can view artefacts from the Bronze Age, trace the history of the Easter Rising, or revisit Leopold Bloom's odyssey in *Ulysses*. Old buildings are being recycled; for example, the 17th-century Royal Hospital at Kilmainham now holds the Museum of Modern Art. And Dublin, a city large in expectations, is still small enough for the visitor to see most of its sights on foot.

City on the Liffey

The River Liffey flows from west to east through the centre of the city to Dublin Bay and forms a natural line between the north and south sections of the city. Historically and culturally this north–south distinction has always been significant, and it still is today, with a dose of good-humoured rivalry between the two areas. 'I never go north of the Liffey,' one man remarked.

Further out, both north and south, are the sweeping curves of the Royal and Grand Canals. The occasional cry of gulls and unexpected distant vistas will remind you that Dublin is by the sea, and that the Wicklow Mountains, which hold Dublin closely to the coast, are within striking distance.

Dublin is an intimate city, physically small but tightly packed, a perfect place for walking. College Green, the home of Trinity College, provides a natural focus just south of O'Connell Bridge. O'Connell Street, the city's grand boulevard, leads north to Parnell Square and the Garden of Remembrance. To the south and east is St

Stephen's Green and the best-preserved Georgian area, where the national museums are located. Along the south bank of the Liffey, to the west, is Temple Bar, up the hill from there are Dublin Castle and Christ Church Cathedral.

Enjoying Dublin

Literature has always flourished in Dublin, the only city to have produced three Nobel Prize for literature winners – Yeats, Shaw and Beckett. Joyce, the high priest of literary Modernism, imagined and interpreted Dublin for the world in *Ulysses* (you'll see references to it everywhere). However, sometimes it seems that the city produced artists of this stature by accident, even against its will. Beckett and Joyce, among others, had to leave their homeland to understand it – and to be understood.

Dublin theatre is legendary, and no visitor should miss seeing a performance at the Abbey Theatre or Gate Theatre. The city's impact on the rock and pop music scene with the likes of U2 and Bob Geldof is well known – there's even a self-guided tour of their haunts. Traditional Irish music is also alive and well, especially in the pubs, where you might easily walk in on a spontaneous live music 'session'. There has, too, been a revival of story-telling, poetry reading and traditional dancing. And in this city, where literature and theatre have historically dominated the scene, visual arts are finally coming into their own, showcased at the

It won't rain on you in Dublin all the time. The climate here can best be described as 'change-able' and yet the sudden shifts from light to dark, sunshine to shower, are part of the city's magic. Buildings seem to transform themselves depending on the light; Dublin under a lowering sky is a different place from Dublin in sunshine.

Museum of Modern Art in Kilmainham, and several cutting-edge galleries in Temple Bar and elsewhere.

Constantly crowded and busy, Grafton Street is the most visible centre for shopping, but retailers all over the city carry an international array of goods as well as the Irish crafts and souvenirs you expect. And while multinational chains have made inroads, they seem less blatant here than elsewhere. Many shops, hotels and guesthouses, have been owned and managed by the same families for years, and theirs is the welcome of traditional Dublin hospitality.

There was a time when you might have apologised for the range and quality of eateries in Dublin, but no longer. The city's food has undergone a metamorphosis, with international restaurants galore, and a New Irish cuisine built upon fresh products of Ireland's seas, rivers and farms. Coffee has replaced the ubiquitous tea – Dublin is now almost as much a coffee city as Vienna or Seattle.

City and Countryside

In a city of such human proportions it is not surprising that parks and gardens abound, perfect for recreation and relaxation. Phoenix Park in the northwest is the largest city park in Europe, but squares like St Stephen's Green are the garden oases of the city.

On the coast, Sandymount, Dollymount and Killiney strands are the places to go. The atmospheric, brooding Wicklow Mountains and the Wicklow Mountains National Park provide a more rugged countryside, and the area has breathtaking houses and gardens such as Castletown, Mount Usher and Powerscourt. To the north and west are several historic sites: Malahide Castle, the evocative hill of Tara, and the long barrows of Knowth and Newgrange.

The DART (Dublin Area Rapid Transit) runs north and south along the coast. It's an ideal way for the visitor to reach outlying sights and villages. There are guided bus tours to sights outside the city.

Young at Heart?

Dublin is a young city. Almost half of Ireland's population is under 25, and with its universities and professional schools, Dublin also has a large student population. The universities attract students from all over the world, and this influx helps to make Dublin a busy, buzzing international city. And young graduates are not leaving now – multinational corporations and European Union investment mean there are plenty of opportunities for them at home. During the rise of the Celtic Tiger (strong economic growth thanks to EU assistance and inclusion), Dublin became a popular place to settle. So popular in fact that the Irish are actually beginning to come home.

Dublin is an old city with a youthful population

A BRIEF HISTORY

Celtic Ireland

Ireland has been inhabited since very ancient times, but Irish history really begins with the arrival of the Celts around the 6th century BC. They brought with them iron weapons, chariots and customs that quickly became dominant in the country. This period sparked myths and legends, later romanticised by Irish writers, that still exercise their power today.

The Celts were organised along a clan-based system, and Celtic Ireland became a series of independent kingdoms. These kingdoms acknowledged an elected High King, with his seat at fabled Tara, as overlord. There were no towns, and the cow was the medium of exchange. Learning was revered, games were played, and the poet was held in awe. Law and religion were important in Celtic culture. The religion was druidic, and the law was an elaborate written code, interpreted by a class of professional lawyers known as *brehons*. The *brehon* laws gave women a high status – they could own property, divorce, and even enter the professions.

Christianity and a Mission to Europe

St Patrick first came to Ireland as a prisoner, captured in an Irish raid on a Roman settlement in Britain. He eventually escaped, but returned to Ireland as a missionary in AD432. By the time of his death in 465, the whole country had been peacefully Christianised, which speaks for Patrick's natural diplomacy as well as his powers of persuasion. Many legends surround his mission. It was St Patrick who used the example of the shamrock to explain the Christian Trinity to King Laoghaire and an assembled crowd at Tara. The king was converted and the plant has been a symbol of Ireland ever since.

With Christianity and the sophisticated Celtic culture successfully fused, Ireland entered its 'Golden Age' (AD500 until around 800). The Irish monasteries became the major preserves of learning and literacy in the so-called 'Dark Ages'. Ireland was 'the light of the known world', sending its saints and scholars out all over Europe.

The Vikings Arrive

Throughout this period, Ireland's political organisation continued much as it had under pagan Celtic rule. There were still no towns; the site of Dublin was only a crossroads, known as *Baile Átha Cliath* ('Town of the Hurdles'; the Irish name is still seen on road signs and buses). From 795, Ireland was repeatedly raided by the Vikings. They sacked the great centres of learning for their treasures and, in the 9th century, built a fort on the Liffey and founded Ireland's first town – *Dubh Linn* or 'Black Pool'. The remains of Viking fortifications can be seen today beneath Dublin Castle. The Vikings also introduced coinage and better ship-building techniques.

In 988 the Irish kings finally united under the King of Munster, Brian Ború, and in a great battle drove the Vikings north of

Medieval manuscript made during Ireland's Golden Age

the Liffey. After this defeat. their influence waned, and they began to be absorbed into the general population. The Irish now held Dublin and in 1038 the first Christ Church Cathedral was founded.

English Rule Begins

In 1169 the Anglo-Normans landed in Wexford, beginning the struggle between England and Ireland that was to dominate Irish history until independence. The Norman incursion began with an internal power struggle. The king of Leinster invited Richard de Clare, known as 'Strongbow', to come to Ireland to help him reclaim his kingdom (Strongbow's tomb can be seen in Christ Church Cathedral). Successive waves of Anglo-Norman invaders followed Strongbow, bringing with them armour, the use of horses in battle, and the feudal system. Unlike the Irish, they favoured centralised administration, and enforced their rule with the building of fortified castles. In 1171 the English king, Henry II, came to Dublin. He granted a charter in 1174 that gave the city rights to free trade. By 1204 Dublin Castle was the centre of English administrative power in Ireland. The city elected its first mayor in 1229, and a parliament was held for the first time in 1297.

Beyond the Pale

The Anglo-Normans, following the pattern of earlier invaders, became rapidly assimilated, though the next two centuries were characterised by repeated attempts by the Irish to rid themselves of their overlords. They were very nearly successful: by the end of the 15th century England held only a small area around Dublin, walled off from the Norman inner city and known as the Pale, with the 'wild Irish' controlling all of the country outside.

All this changed under the Tudors. Henry VIII and Elizabeth I were determined to subdue Ireland, and sent in massive military expeditions. Henry VIII's break with Rome and the Dissolution of the Monasteries meant that by 1558 Dublin's two cathedrals, St Patrick's and Christ Church, had become Protestant (they remain so today). Elizabeth I founded Trinity College in Dublin as a seat of Protestant learning, and it remained just that well into the 20th century.

The Irish continued to resist, but the semi-independent kingdoms were never able to achieve real cohesion. By 1607, they were left leaderless by the 'Flight of the Earls'. The two Ulster earls, O'Neill and O'Donnell went into exile on the Continent, along with many other Irish lords.

From Cromwell to the Boyne

In 1649, Ireland's most hated conqueror, Oliver Cromwell, arrived in Dublin. His ruthless campaigns resulted in more

Founded in 1038, Christ Church Cathedral stands as a symbol of Dublin's rich religious history

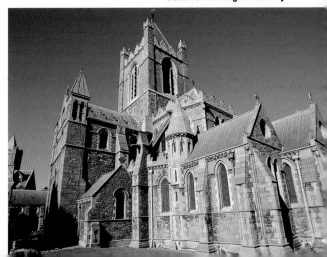

Georgian doors of Dublin

than 600,000 Irish dead or deported. There was a massive dispossession of the Irish from their fertile lands in the east, and they were driven west of the Shannon; in Cromwell's phrase they could go to 'Hell or Connaught'. Some Irish still spit when they hear his name.

At the end of the century, when Catholic king James II came to the throne, the Irish felt they had no choice but to back him. James was defeated by William of Orange just north of Dublin at the Battle of the Boyne in 1690. As a result, the English parliament enacted the Penal Laws of 1704, which disenfranchised Catholics in order to keep the majority of Irish poor and powerless.

Grattan and Wolfe Tone

The 18th century was not a good time for the native Irish, but the Protestant Ascendancy flourished. However, like others before them, they had come to identify themselves as Irish, and they were anxious to achieve at least a measure of self-government for Ireland. In 1782 an Irish parliament was formed in Dublin, largely through the energies of Henry Grattan, MP for the city. Grattan succeeded in having most of the Penal Laws repealed. But the independent parliament was short-lived – against Grattan's opposition, and through bribery and corruption, it voted to dissolve itself in 1800.

In the meantime, the influential ideas of the French Revolution were spreading. The United Irishmen, led by Wolfe Tone, was founded in 1791, a nonsectarian movement that sought the freedom of the Irish people, both Catholic and

Protestant. Wolfe Tone secured aid from France, but a storm scattered the ships of the invading force. Tone was captured and either was murdered or committed suicide. He remains a revered figure in the Irish pantheon.

The Union and O'Connell

Under the Act of Union, Irish members of parliament now served in London. In 1803 there was yet another failed rebellion, led by the great Irish hero Robert Emmet. His speech from the dock and his horrendous execution have become the stuff of legend. Daniel O'Connell carried on the struggle. He formed the peaceful but powerful Catholic Association, and in 1829 the Duke of Wellington, in a bid to avoid a civil war, passed the Catholic Emancipation Bill, which allowed Irish Catholics to sit in the parliament at Westminster for the first time. O'Connell was made Lord Mayor of Dublin in 1841, but failed in his bid to have the Act of Union repealed and an Irish parliament re-established.

Georgian Dublin

The Ascendancy in Dublin enjoyed an elegant lifestyle during this period. Theatre and music flourished. Dublin's importance grew dramatically as the city became the centre of social and business life in Ireland. Craftsmen and architects were imported from Europe and England to create public buildings such as the Custom House and the Four Courts; private mansions like Powerscourt and Leinster House; and Georgian squares like Merrion Square in south Dublin.

The glory of this lively and cosmopolitan city lasted until 1801, when the Act of Union brought Ireland under direct rule from London. Quite suddenly, everything came to a standstill: the rich and powerful left for England, and the city became a provincial capital in a state of long, slow decline.

**These statues at St Stephen's Green commemorate
the 19th-century potato famine**

Famine and Home Rule

The Great Famine struck in 1845 with a blight on the staple
food of the poor, the potato. It lasted until 1848, and it is esti-
mated that more than one million people died and as many
emigrated to escape the ravages of the catastrophe. By the
end of the 1800s, Ireland's population was virtually halved.
Ironically, there was plenty of food around – corn, cattle,
sheep and flour – but it was not available to the poor.

In America a new organisation was formed, the Irish Republican Brotherhood, known as the Fenians. Their rebellion
was aborted, but the society remained active and was influential in the efforts of the National Land League, founded in
1879, which sought to change the tenant system. Charles
Stewart Parnell, an Irish member of parliament, took up the
cause, and the Land Acts, which enabled hard-pressed ten-
ants to buy their land, were passed.

Parnell's other cause was the demand for Home Rule for Ireland. For a time, it looked as if the campaign was going to succeed, but political events, together with the citing of Parnell as co-respondent in a scandalous divorce case, led many to withdraw their support. The bill for Home Rule finally became law just as World War I broke out, but with the proviso that it was not to be enacted until hostilities ended.

The Fight for Freedom

Two years into the war, on Easter Monday, 24 April 1916, armed nationalists, led by trade unionist James Connolly and poet Padraig Pearse, took control of a number of key buildings in the capital. Pearse read out a Declaration of Independence from the General Post Office (GPO) on O'Connell Street. More than 500 people were killed and many buildings damaged – you can see the bullet holes on the GPO building and the Royal College of Surgeons – before the Easter Rising was put down. Fifteen of the leaders were executed, including Pearse and the wounded Connolly, who was brought to his execution in an ambulance and shot tied to a chair. The harshness of the British retribution galvanised the Irish – and in the words of Yeats's poem, 'All changed, changed utterly'. People were no longer content with the prospect of Home Rule – they wanted full independence.

In the general election of 1919 an overwhelming number of Sinn Féin ('Ourselves') republicans were returned to parliament. Instead of going to London, however, they set up a rebel parliament – the first Dáil Éireann – in Dublin, sparking the War of Independence. This guerrilla conflict lasted until 1921, when a treaty was signed giving independence to all of Ireland, except for the six counties of Northern Ireland (where protestant support for the crown was overwhelming). Many republicans baulked at the prospect of only limited independence. Civil war broke out between the supporters of

Michael Collins and Arthur Griffith, who had signed the treaty, and Éamon de Valera's followers who disagreed with the partitioning of the country. A year later, the war was over and the new Irish Free State was born.

Independence and After

In 1937, having made his way back into the Dáil at the head of a new party, de Valera created a republican constitution which took Ireland out of the British Commonwealth. The new republic elected its first president, Douglas Hyde, in 1938. During World War II, though bombs from German planes fell twice on Dublin, the country remained neutral. In 1948, the Irish Republic severed its last ties to Britain.

Neglect, conquest and isolation, however, had taken their toll, and at first independent Ireland was characterised by continued poverty and emigration, a parochial approach to affairs, and domination by the Church.

However, things were about to start looking up: Ireland received huge financial assistance from the European Community, which it joined in 1972, and by the 1990s the economy was beginning to show signs of a boom. The arts began to blossom too. In 1991, Dublin was designated European City of Culture. Musicians such as U2, Enya and Sinead O'Connor put Dublin on the world stage, as – on a smaller scale – did film makers such as Neil Jordan *(The Crying Game)* and Alan Parker *(The Commitments)*.

Ireland has developed into an altogether more forward looking, confident society. In 1990, the dynamic Mary Robinson was chosen as its first woman president. Debates on issues such as divorce and abortion followed, preparing the country for the challenges of the 21st century. In 2002, Ireland was one of the first twelve nations to adopt the euro. As capital of Europe's fastest growing economy today, this new, self-assured Dublin is now very much a European city.

Historical Landmarks

8000 BC First evidence of human habitation in Ireland.

AD 432 St Patrick brings Christianity to Ireland.

AD 795 The Vikings arrive, later building a fort on the Liffey called *Dubh Linn*.

1014 Brian Ború defeats the Vikings at the Battle of Clontarf.

1038 Christ Church established.

1171 Henry II lands at Dublin and claims feudal lordship.

1204 Anglo-Normans rule from Dublin Castle.

1297 First parliamentary sessions in Dublin.

1534 Henry VIII suppresses Catholic Church.

1592 Founding of Trinity College by Elizabeth I.

1649 Oliver Cromwell invades Ireland and devastates the country.

1690 Supporters of Catholic James II defeated at the Battle of the Boyne.

1791 Wolfe Tone's rebellion.

1800 The Irish Parliament is forced to dissolve itself.

1803 Robert Emmet's rebellion and execution.

1829 Daniel O'Connell secures passage of the Catholic Emancipation Act.

1845 Ireland's Great Famine strikes, and lasts until 1848.

1904 Abbey Theatre founded.

1916 The Easter Rising.

1919 Sinn Féin becomes the first Dáil and declares Irish independence.

1919–21 Ireland at war with Britain.

1922 Outbreak of Irish Civil War.

1927 First general election.

1937 Irish constitution adopted.

1938 First president, Douglas Hyde, elected.

1939–45 City bombed by Germany; Ireland remains neutral.

1948 The Republic of Ireland Act severs the last links with Britain.

1955 Ireland joins the United Nations.

1972 Ireland joins the European Economic Community.

1990 Ireland elects its first woman president, Mary Robinson.

1991 Dublin elected European City of Culture.

2002 The euro introduced as Ireland's new unit of currency.

WHERE TO GO

Dublin is a compact city, and many of its important sites are within easy walking distance of one another. There is also a bus service that will take you to attractions away from the city centre. You can get bus information from the Dublin Bus Office in Upper O'Connell Street or from the Dublin Tourism Centre in Suffolk Street. The DART (suburban railway) travels north and south along the coast, a pleasant scenic ride. Car rental is quite expensive, and, with congested traffic and parking problems, is not a good choice within the city, though you may wish to use a car to explore places in the environs *(see pages 68–80)*. There are, however, no shortage of bus tours to outlying destinations.

Your first port of call should be **Dublin Tourism** in Suffolk Street. It is easy to spot, housed in the former St Andrew's Church (open: Mon–Sat 9am–5.30pm); there is also an office in O'Connell Street. You'll find maps, leaflets and other useful information there; you can also arrange accommodation and book tours, theatre tickets and other entertainment. In addition, Dublin Tourism has devised and signposted three self-guided walking tours of the city, which you can follow using the booklets provided. Another good orientation exercise is to start with an organised sightseeing tour with Dublin Bus from Upper O'Connell Street or Bus Éireann from the Travel Centre at Busáras in Store Street.

AROUND GRAFTON STREET

Grafton Street, south of the river, is Dublin's main shopping street. This central pedestrian thoroughfare, enlivened by street entertainers, is lined with stores including Brown

The campanile of Trinity College

Elegant dining at Powerscourt Townhouse Centre

Thomas, Laura Ashley and Marks and Spencer. The original **Bewley's Oriental Café** is here; after 100 years, it is something of an institution and is the best of the many branches across the city. The windows to the rear of its faded art deco ground floor were by stained-glass artist Harry Clarke. It also has a museum and theatre. On the alley by Bewley's is **St Teresa's Church**, with stained-glass windows by Phyllis Burke and a fine sculpture by John Hogan.

A number of more recent shopping complexes are set around Grafton Street. The smart **Powerscourt Townhouse Centre** is probably the most notable of these (a sign points the way just beyond Bewley's to the Clarendon Street entrance). This 1770s mansion was formerly the residence of Viscount Powerscourt and still possesses some magnificent plasterwork, particularly in the rear exit hall. (There are free guided tours of the building on Friday and Saturday at 3pm.) The old house has been tastefully converted, with a pleasant glass-roofed central courtyard surrounded by balconies. There are many cafés and restaurants, and you can shop on the various levels for antiques, crafts and designer clothes. At the top is an art gallery with changing exhibitions. In summer there is a programme of lunchtime recitals.

Next to the shopping centre, at 58 South William Street, is the small and eclectic **Dublin Civic Museum** (open: Tues–Sat 10am–6pm, Sun 11am–2pm, closed Mon; free). This museum offers a sidelong glance at the history of Dublin, with an emphasis on the hidden life of the city and the lesser known people who shaped the life of Dublin. You'll come across old prints, photographs and newspaper clippings, together with old street signs, wooden water mains, coal-hole covers and the original wax models of the river gods on the Custom House. Temporary exhibitions cover subjects ranging from war to writers in Dublin.

Opposite the historical facade of Powerscourt Centre a pathway leads to another historical shopping area. The **George's Street Arcade** is a bustling market selling clothes, food and trinkets and includes an assortment of traditional cafés and coffee shops, all housed under 18th century warehouse arches.

At the top of Grafton Street, where it meets busy Nassau Street, you will see Jean Rynhart's statue of **Molly Malone**, subject of the well-known 18th-century ballad, with her barrow and a very low décolletage. Erected in 1988 to celebrate Dublin's millennium as a city, it has become known to irreverent locals as the 'Tart with the Cart'.

The 'Tart with the Cart' keeps an eye on Grafton Street

Down the street from Molly is the **Bank of Ireland** (guided tours: Tues 10.30am, 11.30am and 1.45pm; chamber open Mon–Fri during banking hours). Constructed in 1729 to house the Irish Parliament, the striking

An Irish Parliament was once housed in the prestigious Bank of Ireland on College Street

building preserves the impressive chamber of the Irish House of Lords with its 18th-century tapestries and coffered ceiling. The building is really a series of additions to an original structure, although the overall effect is one of elegance and superb proportion. The Corinthian portico was designed by James Gandon, who was also responsible for many fine buildings in Georgian Dublin, including the Custom House on the north bank of the Liffey. Plans to house parliament here after Independence came to nothing; Leinster House in Kildare Street was chosen instead.

Behind the bank in Foster Place is the intimate **Bank of Ireland Arts Centre** (open: Tues–Fri 10am–4pm; admission charge). Upstairs is an exhibit on the history of banking and the short-lived Irish Parliament. The centre presents concerts, poetry readings, art exhibitions and various other cultural activities.

Trinity College

Across College Street is **Trinity College**, founded in 1592 to educate the Protestant Anglo-Irish Ascendancy. Only in 1970 did the Catholic Church lift its boycott of the University and proclaim that it was no longer a mortal sin for a Catholic to attend the Protestant university. Today the college is one of the geographical and social hubs of the city, attracting students from around the world. Famous graduates include Jonathan Swift, Oliver Goldsmith, Bram Stoker, Oscar Wilde and Samuel Beckett; resistance heroes Robert Emmet and Wolfe Tone also studied here.

The university sits on College Green, an island of magnificent buildings, open squares and green spaces, surrounded by a sea of traffic. Walk through the gates of the west front, designed by Theodore Jacobsen and built in 1752. The statues on either side are of Edmund Burke and Oliver Goldsmith. You are welcome to explore or take a tour around College Green, but some of the buildings may be closed, depending on the time of year.

Front Square and **Parliament Square**, dating from the 18th century, are surrounded by the Chapel, Dining Hall, Examination Hall and 1937 Reading Room, and anchored by the splendid Campanile. On your left the **Dining Hall**, designed by Richard Castle, has been falling down ever since it was finished in the 1740s and has undergone frequent rebuilding. It was beautifully restored after a damaging fire in 1984. The late 18th-century **Chapel** displays some fine plasterwork and dazzling stained-glass windows, together with a 20th-century organ in an 18th-century case. Opposite the Chapel is the **Examination Hall**, where concerts are given occasionally; otherwise it is rarely open to the public (look through the spy hole in the door). The beautiful stucco ceiling is by Michael Stapleton, who is also responsible for the ceilings in the Dublin Writers Museum.

Among the paintings is a portrait of Archbishop James Usher, who donated the Book of Kells *(see below)* to the University Library. Both the Chapel and Examination Hall were designed by Sir William Chambers, the architect responsible for Marino Casino *(see page 76)*.

The 30-m (100-ft) high **Campanile**, built in 1853 by Sir Charles Lanyon, houses the university's bells. It is impossible to miss the huge *Reclining Connected Forms* by Henry Moore in **Library Square**, or Alexander Calder's *Cactus* behind the Old Library in **Fellows Square**. Architect Paul Koralek's 1967 **Berkeley Library**, fronted by Arnaldo Pomodoro's *Sphere Within Sphere*, fits seamlessly into the earlier buildings. The eastern side of the square once housed Oliver Goldsmith's rooms; renovated in Victorian times, little of the original building remains.

A combined ticket provides admission to the Book of Kells and the Dublin Experience. Guided tours – often led by students earning their bread – sometimes include admission charges, as well as providing a more personal exploration of the campus.

Trinity's most important possession is the 9th-century **Book of Kells**. The exhibition, 'Turning Darkness into Light' (open Oct–May: Mon–Sat 9.30am–5pm, Sun noon–4.30pm; June–Sept: daily 9.30am–4.30pm; admission charge), is in the **Colonnades** beneath the Old Library. It begins with a series of lighted panels illustrating the manuscript. The book itself is displayed along with other illuminated manuscripts such as the Book of Durrow or the Book of Armagh; pages of the books are turned every six weeks. The exhibition is tremendously popular, so be prepared for some long queues at the entrance.

Upstairs is the impressive **Long Room**, or Old Library, opened in 1732. A barrel-ceilinged chamber 64m (209ft) long, with windows along both sides, it holds Trinity's oldest books, including a Shakespeare folio. There is an elaborate gift shop at the entrance to the exhibition.

Across Fellows' Square in the modern Arts Building, the **Dublin Experience** (45-minute shows daily, on the hour 10am–5pm; admission charge), a wide-screen audio-visual show about the history of Dublin, provides a good introduction for those unfamiliar with Irish culture or Dublin's history.

Also in the Arts Building is the airy **Douglas Hyde Gallery** (open: Mon–Fri 11am–6pm, Thur until 7pm; Sat 11am–4.45pm; free), a

The grand front entrance to Trinity College

modern two-level exhibition space and the place to go for the cutting edge in Irish and international art.

The Samuel Beckett Theatre and the Players Theatre provide budding students with a stage on which to shine. Both are located in the **Samuel Beckett Centre** and produce an array of student productions with the occasional touring show.

If you'd like to see college life in action – and the weather's good – make your way to the **Pavillion** on College Park, at the opposite end of campus to the main gates. It serves student-priced drinks and is surrounded by green spaces that sprout many a sunning student on a warm day. It's a great place to relax, watch the rugby team practice and hear others fret over upcoming exams. If the weather's cold, try the **Buttery** under the Dining Hall building – an eatery and bar in the basement that's low on comfort, but full of high jinx.

Dawson and Kildare Streets

From College Green head down Nassau Street (site of many craft and souvenir shops), then turn right into Dawson Street. Here you'll find bookshops, boutiques and another shopping complex, this one built on the site of the Royal Hibernian Hotel and naturally called the **Royal Hibernian Way**.

   St Anne's Church (facing Anne Street South) has some colourful 19th-century stained glass, and provides the setting for lunchtime concerts (look for the notices in the vestibule). A few doors down is the charming **Mansion House**, official residence of the mayor of Dublin since 1715. The house was built in 1710 for a property speculator, one Joshua Dawson, after whom the street was named. Behind it is the **Round Room**, where in 1919 the Irish parliament adopted the Declaration of Independence.

Café on trendy Anne Street South

   Turn down Molesworth Street, lined with several fine-art galleries, to reach Kildare Street, where you will see the elegant entrance to **Leinster House**, once owned by the earls of Kildare, and now home to the Irish parliament. This building is believed by some to have provided the basis for the design of Washington's White House in the United States, designed by Irish architect James Hoban in 1870. It is open to the public when parliament is not sitting. On the west side of the street is the entrance to the **National Library** and next to it is a branch of the Na-

Leinster House, seat of Ireland's Parliament

tional Museum *(see below)*. Tickets are required for the reading rooms of the library, but can be obtained during office hours (10am–5pm, closed noon–2pm). Over half a million items here provide a vast archive of the nation. Exhibitions are often held in the splendid entrance hall (open: Mon–Wed 10am–9pm, Tues–Fri 10am–5pm, Sat 10am–1pm).

The Museum of Archaeology and History located on Kildare Street is just one of four branches belonging to the **National Museum**, Dublin's most important historic collection. The other branches include the nearby Museum of Natural History; Collins Barracks near Phoenix Park, which is linked by a free bus service; and the Museum of Country Life in Castlebar, in County Mayo. All are free and found on the museum's website (<www.museum.ie>).

The **Museum of Archaeology and History** (open: Tues–Sat 10am–5pm, Sun 2–5pm, closed Mon; guided tours take 40 minutes and depart regularly) contains Bronze-Age Irish gold and other archaeological finds. Opened in 1890, the building itself is noteworthy for its entrance hall and Rotunda, mosaic floors and the elaborate blue-and-yellow majolica decoration on the pediments and jambs of the doors. The exhibits are state-of-the art. **Ór: Ireland's Gold** displays the astonishing accomplishments of goldsmiths from 2000 to 700BC. Medieval treasures include the famous Ardagh Chalice and Tara Brooch, along with metalwork from the Viking period. The museum also has a small Egyptian gallery and an exhibit focusing on the history of Irish independence. There is also a good, but crowded café and a small gift shop.

Deane & Woodward, the architects responsible for the library and museum, also built the Kildare Street Club, in 1861. This marvellous Victorian-Gothic building is famous for the fanciful stone carvings around the base of its pillars (one pillar, reputedly depicting the club members, shows monkeys playing billiards). The club itself was a bastion of Ascendancy establishment. The building now houses the

Finding Your Ancestors

If you have an Irish last name or Irish ancestry, you may want to join the crowd that comes to Ireland ancestor hunting. Your grandmother's family stories may be the clue – begin at home by collecting family names.

Dublin is a good place to start your search. The Genealogical Office in Kildare Street is the best source for information on family names, and the National Library next door has a large collection of genealogical and historical records. Other sources are the Office of the Registrar General in the Custom House, with records of Protestant marriages, births and deaths going back to 1845 and Catholic records from 1861; the Record Office of the Four Courts; and the Registry of the Deeds, in Henrietta Street. If you know the county your family came from, or better still, the town or village, you can go directly to the appropriate parish registers; these go back more than 200 years. Churchyard monuments and gravestones can also be a source of information.

Heraldic Museum and Genealogical Office (open: Mon–Wed 10am–8.30pm, Thur–Fri 10am–4pm, Sat 10am–12.30pm and 2.30–4.30pm; free), with exhibits on the history of heraldry. The consulting service of the office of Ireland's Chief Herald will help you trace your own ancestry, and if you qualify and have the requisite cash to spare, you can

Ornamental street lamp

apply for a Grant of Arms. Just opposite this bastion of Irish heritage is another, namely **Am Bia**, the only Irish speaking coffee shop in Dublin.

Around St Stephen's Green

Walk to the bottom of Kildare Street and you will reach **St Stephen's Green**, formerly an open common, but enclosed in 1663 and now a 9-hectare (22-acre) park in the heart of the city, surrounded by some beautiful buildings. Although formally laid out as a public park only in 1877–80, it is the oldest green in Dublin, dating back to medieval times. A popular and often crowded place, the Green contains large formal lawns with ornate gardens, duck ponds, a bandstand and a children's playground.

Entering the park from St Stephen's Green North you will come across the **Wolfe Tone Memorial** opposite the famous Shelbourne Hotel (1824), and behind it a work entitled *Famine*, both by sculptor Edward Delaney. The ***Three Fates*** fountain is a monument to the Irish spirit. Presented by Germany in thanks to the Irish who opened their country to orphaned German children after World War II, the three forlorn

Inside the St Stephen's Green Shopping Centre

figures face Earlsfort Terrace, twisting a piece of string representing fate. Facing St Stephen's Green South is Marjorie Fitzgibbon's bust of **James Joyce**. Working your way around the park, you will see the 1907 **Fusilier's Arch** at the Grafton Street corner.

The **St Stephen's Green Shopping Centre** at the south end of Grafton Street, a pseudo-Victorian iron-and-glass structure, was built in the 1980s, and has been christened 'The Wedding Cake' by Dubliners. It houses a wide selection of shops and stalls as well as a pub and restaurant on the top floor, under the glass dome.

Halfway down the west side of the green is the massive Georgian **Royal College of Surgeons**, built in 1806. Those chips in the stonework are bullet holes from the 1916 Easter Rising — the building was occupied by independence fighters led by Countess Markievicz.

One of Dublin's best-kept secrets is the **Iveagh Gardens**, accessible from Clonmel Street via Harcourt Street or from behind the National Concert Hall off Earlsfort Terrace. Neither entrance is obvious, hence the gardens' sense of seclusion. Designed as a series of pleasure gardens in the Italianate style in 1863, with cascades, spectacular fountains, and rustic grottoes, the gardens were opened to the public in 1991.

The Georgian curve of Harcourt Street (constructed in 1775) was once home to George Bernard Shaw (nos. 60–61). The **Shaw Birthplace Museum** at 33 Synge Street (open May–Oct: Mon–Sat 10am–5pm, Sun 11am–5pm; admission charge), is marked by a plaque written by the great man himself. This Victorian house where he spent his early years has exhibits on Shaw and the Dublin he knew. It is furnished as a small but charming Dublin household typical of the period. Tours and booklets are available in a number of languages, and the staff are very friendly.

From here it is a short walk, following the signs, to the small **Irish-Jewish Museum** (open May–Sept: Tues, Thur and Sun 11am–3pm; Oct–Apr: Sun 10.30am–2.30pm) in Walworth Road. This former synagogue, set in the heart of what was the city's Jewish quarter in the late 19th/early 20th century, tells the story of the Jews in Ireland by means of documents, memorabilia and old photographs, revealing a little-known part of Dublin's community. (Look for a Guinness bottle with a Hebrew label.)

Back along the south side of St Stephen's Green begins a fine array of buildings. The first of these is the **University Church**, built in 1853 by Cardinal Henry Newman, then rector of University College Dublin (UCD). The strangely compelling Byzantine-style interior is a very popular venue for weddings.

Enjoying a stroll on the Green

Next door, nos. 85 and 86 comprise the exquisite **Newman House**, part of University College (guided tours June–Aug: Tues–Fri noon–5pm, Sat 2–5pm, Sun

The Newman House contains rococo busts of man and beast

11am–2pm, closed Mon; admission charge). Number 85 dates from 1740 and contains the famous Apollo Room, with panels depicting Apollo and the muses, and the magnificent rococo salon, both by the La Francini brothers, who also worked on Russborough House *(see page 73)*. Number 86 next door, largely the work of Robert West, has even more elaborate ornamentation.

James Joyce was a student here, and, towards the end of his life, the poet Gerard Manley Hopkins lectured here. One of the classrooms Joyce attended can be seen on the guided tour, and Hopkins's room has been restored. There is a very pleasant terrace and in the basement is The Commons, which ranks among the best restaurants in Dublin.

Just beyond Newman House is **Iveagh House**, home to the Irish government's Department of Foreign Affairs, but closed to the public. Both Newman House and Iveagh House were designed by Richard Castle.

Beyond Iveagh House in Earlsfort Terrace (turn south) is the **National Concert Hall**, of impressive proportions and uncertain acoustics – it's a conversion of an old Examination Hall of University College.

Back at the northeast corner of St Stephen's Green, near the Shelbourne Hotel, you can turn right into Merrion Row to peer through the railings at the small **Huguenot Cemetery** (no entry to visitors). The cemetery dates back to 1693, when French Protestants, fleeing persecution in their native land, settled in Dublin, bringing with them their architectural and weaving skills, which greatly enriched their adopted city.

At the end of Ely Place, which runs south from Merrion Row and Baggot Street, is the **Royal Hibernian Academy** (open: Tues–Sat 11am–5pm, Thur until 8pm, Sun 2–5pm), where temporary contemporary art shows are held.

OLD DUBLIN

West of O'Connell Street, around Christ Church Cathedral, is the site of the original Viking town of *Dubh Linn*, which developed eastwards along the river towards Trinity College. In 1592, when Trinity was built, it was not in but near Dublin.

Temple Bar

Between the river and Dame Street is **Temple Bar**, once a run-down area but now a firm fixture on the tourist map, famous for its nightlife and streetlife. Along the narrow cobbled lanes dating from the 18th century – partly pedestrianised and fairly free of traffic – you will find some original architecture, and many lively pubs, clubs, cafés, alternative shops and restaurants. Temple Bar is also home to a wealth of artists and musicians, and there are crafts and art workshops, galleries and music centres.

You can enter Temple Bar from Dame Street, or from Fleet Street (off Westmoreland Street), or you can walk through **Merchants Arch**, opposite the picturesque arching Ha'penny Bridge, into Temple Bar Square. Continuing along Temple Bar, you'll come to Eustace Street and Meeting House Square. Most of the cultural centres that make Temple Bar interesting are located in this area. The **Irish Film Centre** *(see page 93–4)* in Eustace Street opened in 1992 and is the main outlet for arthouse and foreign films. It maintains a popular café/bar and its shop has a good selection of posters and books on film theory. Also in Eustace Street is an information office and a cultural centre for children, **The Ark** *(see page 96)*.

On Meeting House Square is the **Gallery of Photography** (open: Tues–Sat 11am–6pm; free), displaying photographs of Dublin past and present alongside changing exhibitions of Irish and international photography. There are also books and posters for sale.

The **National Photo Archive** (open: Mon–Fri 10am–5pm, Sat 10am–2pm; free), also located on Meeting House Square, maintains the photographic collections of the National Library of Ireland. The archive provides reading rooms for research and puts on temporary exhibitions.

On Curved Street, the **Arthouse Multimedia Centre for the Arts** (open: Mon–Fri, 10am–5.30pm; free) brings art and multimedia together through exhibitions, courses and workshops. Across the street the **Temple Bar Music Centre** is a resource centre for music, media and stage production *(see page 93)*. The **Project Arts Centre** (39 East Essex Street) displays avant-garde painting and sculpture and also has a performance space upstairs.

On Dame Street, Temple Bar's southern boundary, is a gem of Victorian architecture: the **Olympia Theatre** *(see page 93)*. Built in 1870, its canopy of stained glass and cast iron is the oldest in Dublin; its enthusiastic interior decoration is also typical of the era. Happily, the restored theatre leads a

**The Streets are aglow after the Irish sun has set.
On Thursdays, many shops stay open late**

bustling, active life, with a regular schedule of light hearted
plays and concerts. Just across the way is **City Hall**, built
originally as the Royal Exchange in 1769–79. This fine building with its Corinthian portico was designed by Thomas Coo-
ley. The **Story of the Capital** (open: Mon–Sat 10am–
5.15pm, Sun 2–5pm; admission charge; guided tours of City
Hall also available) traces the history of Dublin over the last
1,000 years). Just to the west of City Hall lies one of Dublin's
most important historic sites, Dublin Castle.

Dublin Castle

Today, as you walk through the Great Gate into the spacious
Georgian yard, **Dublin Castle** (guided tours: Mon–Fri
10am–5pm, Sat–Sun 2–5pm; admission charge) looks both
serene and imposing. For seven centuries the real and sym-
bolic centre of British military and social power, it is a mon-

ument that still has resonance for Dubliners. The castle has been built and rebuilt several times over the course of its history, and little remains of the original Anglo-Norman structure that was built in 1204. It sits on the site of the *Dubh Linn* (Black Pool) that gave Dublin its name.

The guided tour commences with the **State Apartments** on the south side of the building. Lavishly furnished and decorated, with much original period furniture, the rooms are used for ceremonial events, visits from foreign dignitaries, and EU meetings. The **Connolly Room** is so called because it was here that the wounded James Connolly spent his last night before being executed for his part in the Easter Rising. You may notice the exquisite ceiling in the **Granard Room**. It was moved here from Mespil House and is called the 'Hibernia Ceiling'. The **Drawing Room** was partially destroyed by fire in 1941, and its furnishings are faithful reproductions; the huge (repaired) Ming punch bowl is striking.

A splendid carpet, with a design based on a page from the Book of Kells *(see page 28)*, covers the floor of the **Throne Room**. The rather large throne was last used in 1911 by George V. In the lovely **Picture Gallery**, convex wall mirrors made it possible for the host at table to keep his eye on everyone,

Relaxing outside Dublin Castle

The Legend of British Justice

Above the main gate of Dublin Castle stands a statue of Justice. The fact that it has it's back turned to the city was seen by Dubliners as an apt symbol of British rule. The farce doesn't end there though. This Justice, thanks to the naivety of the sculptor, has no blindfold. Furthermore the statue, inadvertantly of course, drained rainwater from the head, down the arm and into the the metal scales she holds, tipping them out of balance.

particularly the servants. The **Wedgewood Room** contains a Phoenix carpet given by de Valera, and plaques by English sculptor John Flaxman and Danish sculptor Berthel Thorwaldsen. The enormous **St Patrick's Hall**, with its painted ceiling by Vincenzo Valdre, contains the banners and coats of arms of the now-defunct Knights of St Patrick. The hall is now used for the inauguration of the Irish president.

One of the most interesting parts of the tour is the underground excavation of the **Viking and Norman Defences**. Visitors can stand in the dry bed of the old moat, traverse imaginative gangways over the encroaching river (the Poddle, not the Liffey), and view the stairs at which boats once landed provisions for the castle. In the restored **Treasury** (built in 1715, located in the Lower Yard), browse in the bookshop or relax in the Castle Vaults Bistro and Patisserie.

The oldest remaining part of the castle is the **Record Tower** (1258), visible as you leave the upper yard. The Gothic-revival 19th-century **Church of the Most Holy Trinity**, adjacent to the tower, has stone work by Edward Smyth and a fan-vaulted ceiling. The Crypt Arts Centre is under the church and presents exhibitions, plays and concerts.

A recent addition to the castle precinct is the **Chester Beatty Library** (open May–Sept: Mon–Fri 10am–5pm, Sat 11am–5pm, Sun 1–5pm; Oct–Apr: Tues–Fri 10am–5pm;

Detail from the exterior of Dublin Castle

free), which moved here from Ballsbridge. It is a treasure house of Islamic manuscripts, Chinese, Japanese and Indian art and texts. Biblical papyri and Christian manuscripts are also on display, completing one of the richest collections of the written word in Western and Eastern cultures. The library itself includes copies of the Koran and codices dating from the second century BC. This superb collection rightfully won the European Museum of the Year award in 2002.

Christ Church Cathedral and Environs

Further up the hill on Castle Street from the Great Gate is the first of Dublin's two major cathedrals, **Christ Church Cathedral** in Christchurch Place (open: Mon–Fri 9.45am–5pm, Sat–Sun 10am–5pm; donation suggested). Standing, like the castle, on a hill, the cathedral rises on the site of King Sitric's 11th-century wooden church. The foundations date back to 1172 when 'Strongbow', the Earl of Pembroke, had it rebuilt as a stone structure. By 1558, after Henry VIII's break with the Roman Catholic Church, all the existing foundations in Dublin had become Anglican (see page 15).

Unfortunately, the church building was massively and unsympathetically restored in 1871–8, when most of the original interior was ripped out. However, there is still much to appreciate in Christ Church, including the impressive stonework, soaring nave, and the handsome 19th-century encaustic floor tiles based on a 13th-century pattern. Strongbow's tomb is in the church; and in the **Peace Chapel** is a somewhat macabre artefact – the embalmed heart of St Lawrence O'Toole, the influential 12th-century archbishop of Dublin, which is kept in a cage suspended on the wall near the altar. The cathedral choir traces its origins back to 1480 and has the distinction of taking part in the world's first ever performance of Handel's Messiah. Choral Evensong is on Wednesdays and Thursdays at 6pm.

The vast, vaulted medieval crypt is the oldest structure in Dublin. An exhibition, entitled **Treasures of Christ Church**, takes up much of the crypt. An additional charge is required to see this limited number of ancient texts, plus the tabernacle of James II, a William of Orange plate, commemorating his victory in the Battle of the Boyne, and a 1666 Common Prayer Book. In the open areas of the crypt, amongst the forest of heavy stone pillars are a few items of note, including stocks dating from 1670, medieval carved stones and a curious exhibit – a mum mified cat and a rat, found trapped in the organ pipes.

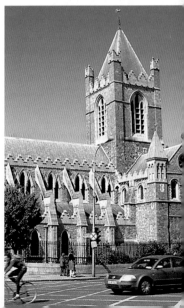

Christ Church Cathedral

In the Old Synod Hall, just across the road from the cathedral (and linked to it by a bridge), you will find **Dublinia** (open Apr–Sept: daily 10am–5pm; Oct–Mar: Mon–Sat 11am–4pm, Sun 10am–4.30pm; admission

You don't have to search very hard for Vikings in Dublin's history

charge), a sight-and-sound re-creation (in five languages) of Dublin in medieval times. You can walk through the streets of the old city, experience the sights and sounds of a medieval market and visit a Merchant's House. Upstairs is a gift shop and the entrance to the connecting walkway to the cathedral; you can climb the tower, which has an interesting view of the surroundings.

Wood Quay, on the south bank of the river (downhill from the arch and dominated by the featureless offices of the Dublin Corporation) is the site of the original Viking settlement. Unfortunately, the construction of these offices obliterated much of the archaeological dig that unearthed the original layout of the 9th-century quay, but the Viking artefacts that were found are on view in the National Museum *(see page 31)*.

A short distance from the cathedral on High Street are the two **St Audoen's churches**. The restored Church of Ireland St Audoen's is the older of the two (*circa* 1190) and is the only remaining medieval church in the city (tours June–Sept: daily 9.30am–5.30pm; admission charge). Next door is the narrow, lofty neoclassical facade of Catholic St Audoen's, built in 1847. Both churches stand beside what remains of the old city walls, and St Audoen's is the only surviving gate. In medieval times the High Cross of the Norman city, where decrees and notices of excommunication were read out, stood on the High Street. Granite markers erected in 1991 indicate the line of the old city walls.

West from here in Thomas Street, a plaque on the decommissioned and forlorn-looking **St Catherine's Church** (built in 1769) marks the spot where the famed Irish resistance hero Robert Emmet was hanged in 1803. **John's Lane Church** further down Thomas Street is more remarkable. Though just over 100 years old, it is one of the most attractive churches in the city. Thomas Street West becomes James's Street, where the **Guinness Brewery** has been situated ever since 1759.

Guinness Brewery and Environs

Well west of the city centre lie several of Dublin's top tourist attractions. Handily, they are all clustered near Heuston Station, which is well serviced by bus from the centre. The **Guinness Storehouse** is the latest incarnation of the Guinness Brewery tour – and an ultra-modern one at that. This self-guided tour begins on the ground level with ingredients

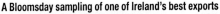

A Bloomsday sampling of one of Ireland's best exports

and ends in the very stylish Gravity bar atop the brewery with a 360 degree view of Dublin and the freshest (and free-est) pint of Guinness in town. Along the way you get to see and sniff the various stages of the brewing process. Despite all the entertaining technology, the tour is ultimately educational, as you watch films of old coopers making the casks for the brew and just how Guinness is created from the four simple ingredients of water, barley, hops and yeast.

The restored Royal Hospital at Kilmainham, which now houses the **Irish Museum of Modern Art** (open: Tues–Sat 10am–5.30pm, Sun noon–5.30pm, closed Mon; free) is Dublin's most important 17th-century building (1684) and is worth a visit for its own sake. With its wonderful light and space, it makes a tremendous exhibition area. The museum's holdings include the Gordon Lambert Collection, with more than 100 works dating from the 1960s–70s. The real attraction, however, are the numerous temporary exhibits that the museum hosts. There is an international residency programme for artists, and visitors may meet the artists in their studios (depending on schedules). Concerts and special events are also held in the museum, and there is an atmospheric café in the vaults.

A stage in the Guinness brewing process

Further west is the evocative museum of the **Kilmainham Gaol** (open: daily 9.30am–6pm, shorter hours in winter; admission charge). Kilmainham was the major Irish prison for well over a century, with Éamon de Valera as its last prisoner in 1924. An excellent exhibition traces the history of the

Learn about life behind bars at Kilmainham Gaol, which held criminals and political prisoners alike until 1924

prison (including a section on Victorian theories about prisons and the treatment of prisoners), as well as the political and social events that brought many of the prisoners here. A 25-minute audio-visual presentation in the prison chapel is followed by a guided tour through the dark corridors of the 18th-century part of the building, where you can see the cells occupied by those who took part in the Easter Rising – they were executed in the prison yard.

Nearby, on the south bank of the Liffey, is the **Irish National War Memorial Park**, constructed during the 1930s to designs by the architect and landscape designer Edwin Lutyens. The gardens are a tribute to the thousands of Irish soldiers who died in World War I while serving in the British Army. The sombre design incorporates the War Stone and four granite pavilions, one of which contains Celtic and art deco illuminated manuscripts by Harry

Tailors' Hall, home of An Taisce

Clarke, listing the names of those killed in action.

On the north bank of the Liffey, behind Wolfe Tone Quay, are the former **Collins Barracks** (open: Tues–Sat 10am–5pm, Sun 2–5pm; free). Built in 1701, the barracks were occupied continuously until they were decommissioned in 1997. Since then, they have been home to the National Museum's collection of decorative arts. Silver, ceramics, furniture and folk artefacts trace Ireland's social and political history. There is also a café, bookshop and parking.

The Liberties

Back towards the city centre now, and to the south of High Street, the area known as the **Liberties** was so named because it was situated outside the medieval city walls and was run by local courts, free of city regulations on trade. The area, once a slum, is rapidly gentrifying, with new housing and restoration of the original small red-brick houses.

Across from the two St Audoen's *(see page 44)*, two interesting streets run off High Street. **Francis Street** is lined with antiques shops, full of glittering treasures, and in **Back Lane** are the headquarters of An Taisce, an organisation dedicated to the preservation of historic buildings and gardens in Ireland. Appropriately, its home is the delightful **Tailors' Hall**, the oldest guildhall in Ireland, once used by hosier and barber-surgeons' guilds as well as by the tailors. It dates from 1706, and is one of the few remaining original Queen Anne buildings in Dublin.

St Patrick's Cathedral

At the eastern end of Back Lane and turning right, Nicholas Street becomes Patrick Street. On the left, off St Patrick's Close, is **St Patrick's Cathedral** (open: Mon–Fri 9am–6pm; Sat 9am–5pm, Sun 10am–6pm; admission charge). This is the oldest Christian site in Dublin – St Patrick himself is reputed to have baptised converts on this spot (marked by a Celtic cross in the nave), suggesting that there has been a church here since around AD450. In the adjoining St Patrick's Park is a marker showing the site of **St Patrick's Well**.

The height and space of the cathedral are impressive. Note the carved helmets and swords set above the choir stalls and the 19th-century tiled floor, similar to the one in Christ Church. The 90-m (300-ft) interior makes it the longest church in the country. The 45-m (150-ft) tower holds the largest ringing peal of bells in Ireland. Not much is left of the original construction of 1191: Destroyed in a fire in the 14th century, it was later rebuilt, and even includes some Victorian restoration work, though not as extensive as that in Christ Church.

The cathedral has had a varied history. From 1320, until it was closed by Henry VIII, St Patrick's was the seat of Ireland's first university. Later, Cromwellian

St Patrick's Cathedral

troops used the aisles to stable their horses. The great Jonathan Swift, author of *Gulliver's Travels*, was dean here from 1713 to 1745. He was much revered for his charity and his championship of the Irish cause. You can see his grave and that of his great love, Esther Johnson, as well as the pulpit from which he preached. On the wall is his epitaph, written by himself.

An interesting artefact from the medieval chapter house is a door with a hole in it. The hole was cut in 1492 by Lord Kildare so he could reassure his arch enemy Lord Ormonde, who was under siege in the chapter house, of his friendly intentions. Kildare put his arm through the hole, thus giving rise to the common expression 'to chance your arm'.

Also in St Patrick's Close (left from the cathedral exit) is **Marsh's Library** (open: Mon and Wed–Fri 10am–12.45pm and 2–5pm, Sat 10.30am–12.45pm; donations suggested),

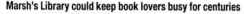

Marsh's Library could keep book lovers busy for centuries

the first public library in Ireland, founded in 1701 and holding more than 25,000 books, most dating from the 16th to the 18th century. The oak shelving is original, as are the metal cages in which scholars were locked so as to prevent thefts. Even if you aren't a scholar, do come here – the atmosphere and beauty of the place is entrancing.

GEORGIAN DUBLIN

Much of the surviving architecture of Dublin comes from the Georgian period. It may seem somewhat arbitrary to designate one area of the city as 'Georgian' – Georgian architecture is found all over the city; however, the harmonious streets and squares lying to the southeast of Nassau Street truly deserve the title. In addition to the superb buildings, there are several important museums and galleries to visit, and the banks of the Grand Canal provide leafy, shaded walks.

Merrion Square

Clare Street, at the eastern end of Nassau Street, runs into **Merrion Square North**, where you'll find some of the finest houses. The square dates from 1762; houses here were the homes of high society, including many members of parliament and famous artists and writers. Look for individual details on the houses – the painted doors, the fan lights, and the door knockers, some in the form of a fish or a human hand.

On Merrion Square West is the National Gallery of Ireland, which provides tickets for free 40-minute tours of the restored **Government Buildings** (tours: Sat 10.30am–3.30pm; no pre-booking required) in Upper Merrion Street. Refurbished in 1990–91 and housing the offices and meeting rooms of the *Taoiseach* (Prime Minister) and his cabinet, the interior rooms of the buildings are a fascinating and tasteful combination of the old and the new. Along with the latest technology, the *Taoiseach*'s office has a superb Bossi marble fireplace, and a fine display of art and crafts.

A magnificent Evie Hone stained-glass window adorns the landing in the main entrance; it is beautifully complemented by the carpet and balustrade designed by Mary Fitzgerald. There is some excellent contemporary furniture and a miniature of Oisín Kelly's sculpture *The Children of Lir*. Outside, the courtyard is paved in limestone tram-setts from the streets of Old Dublin.

Also in Merrion Street, next to the front garden of Leinster House, is the Victorian collection of the **Natural History Museum** (open: Tues–Sat 10am–5pm, Sun 2–5pm; free). This Victorian museum, opened in 1857 (with a speech by Dr Livingstone no less), holds a comprehensive collection of Ireland's and the world's zoology. Two giant Irish Deer

The Natural History Museum holds lessons about the many creatures of Ireland for pupils of all ages

skeletons are one of the first things you see. The cabinets are stuffed with mammals, birds, fish, butterflies and insects – it's popularly known as the 'Dead Zoo.' A favourite with children, it gives a fascinating glimpse into the late-Victorian obsession with travelling and collecting.

The **National Gallery** (open: Mon–Sat 9.30am–5.30pm, Thur until 8.30pm, Sun noon–5pm; free) houses a fine collection of works from the 14th to the 20th century – from Goya, Brueghel, Titian, Velasquez, Rembrandt and Gainsborough, to Monet, Degas and Picasso. One of the gallery's most important paintings, on permanent loan from the Jesuit Brothers in whose house it was discovered in 1993, is Caravaggio's long-lost masterpiece, *The Taking of Christ*.

There is a notable collection of Irish art, including a roomful of Jack Yeats's paintings. There are also watercolours, drawings, prints, sculpture and a multimedia gallery, where a computerised system offers information about 100 of the gallery's best works. With a good bookshop and the excellent Fitzer's café you could easily spend a day here. The Millennium Wing, a new 13,500-sq-m (44,000-sq-ft) extension to the museum, opened in 2002 and is used mostly for temporary exhibitions.

> **The addition of the Millennium Wing has made the National Gallery a truly modern institution, but this was not always the case. In the late 1980s, the museum was in such a state of disrepair, one art-lover was able to steal a small French oil painting and post it back to the gallery in protest at the lack of care taken with the artworks.**

Enter one of the many gates of **Merrion Square Park** and walk along some of the secret, wooded paths to the immaculately groomed gardens. Don't miss Danny Osborne's statue of Oscar Wilde, wearing a smoking jacket with red lapels and reclining on a rock in the northeast corner of the park. At the height of the Great Famine in 1845–7, a soup kitchen was set up here to feed the starving. You'll want to return here to browse the **Boulevard Galleries** of art set up around the square on summer weekends.

Fitzwilliam Square and Ballsbridge

Take time to stroll down the streets around Merrion Square, which were laid out at the same time as the square. At the eastern end of Upper Mount Street you'll notice the distinctive shape of the Greek-revival **St Stephen's Church**, which dates back to 1824. For obvious reasons it is known universally as the 'Pepper Canister Church'; occasional events and concerts are held here.

Lower Fitzwilliam Street, at the southeast corner of Merrion Square, houses the offices of the Electricity Supply

Crossing Fitzwilliam Square in style

Board. They tried to make up for the ugliness of their new premises by restoring **Number Twenty Nine** (open: Tues–Sat 10am–5pm, Sun 2–5pm; admission charge) as a museum representing a typical bourgeois house of the period. And indeed, this lovely Georgian townhouse has been superbly fitted out to reflect middle-class life in the late 18th to early 19th century. An audio-visual display, cosily narrated by the 'ghost' of the former owner and her much put-upon maidservant, is followed by a half-hour guided tour for a maximum of ten people. The staff are friendly and helpful, and there is a small tearoom. The place can get very busy, though.

The street crosses Lower Baggot Street and leads on to **Fitzwilliam Square**, which has a park open to residents only. The last of Dublin's Georgian squares to be built, it was completed by 1830, although the older houses date back to 1714. Here, as elsewhere in Georgian Dublin, there is exquisite detail in the doorways and fanlights, and the ironwork of the balconies.

Back in Baggot Street is the main office of the Bank of Ireland. The road was named after Baggotrath Castle, which stood here until the early 19th century. At Baggot Street Bridge you will find the headquarters of Bord Fáilte (the Irish Tourist Board). If you turn right along the towpath of the canal, you can see the Irish poet Patrick Kavanagh, who died in 1967, preserved in bronze and relaxing on a bench.

> Patrick Kavanagh was born in 1904 at Mucker, Inniskeen, County Monaghan. His father eeked a living from the land and by reparing the shoes that walked upon it. Young Patrick joined in these trades with little success. Local farmers made a joke of his farming skills and called him a fool for pursuing poetry. He moved to Dublin and in 1936 Tarry Flynn, his first publication, set his reputation on its way.

The **Grand Canal** was begun in 1755. The pleasant tow-path walk, under a canopy of leaves, goes past the gardens of terraced houses, offices and apartment buildings. There are plenty of ducks, moorhens and swans, and the canal is spanned by the very distinctive curves of the 18th-century bridges. This is a good place to rest and recuperate, and gain a different slant on life in the city; you may come upon the Barge Café, which travels up and down the canal, and serves breakfast and brown-bag lunches. If you want more information about the canals, you can visit the **Waterways Visitor Centre** (open June–Sept: daily 9.30am–6.30pm; Oct–May: 12.30–5pm; admission charge), on Grand Canal Quay. Opened in 1993, this exciting and imaginative small centre is built on piers over the waters of the canal. The exhibition includes working models and displays devoted to the history and ecology of Ireland's canals. Opposite the centre and set in a restored sugar mill is the **Tower Crafts Design Centre**, comprising shops, workshops, and a first-floor restaurant.

Beyond Baggot Street Bridge to the east is the suburb of **Ballsbridge**, at the heart of which are the grounds of the **Royal Dublin Society** (RDS) where the famous Dublin (Kerrygold) Horse Show takes place. The society was founded in 1731, and established among other things, the National Gallery and the National Library. All sorts of events and concerts are held at the showground. On the corner of Elgin and Pembroke Road is the American Embassy, a curious round building, conceived by a partnership of an American and an Irish architect in 1964.

NORTH OF THE RIVER

Dublin north of the Liffey has its own atmosphere and, like the southern part of the city, some magnificent buildings, museums, and Dublin's two most important theatres, the Abbey and the Gate.

Crossing **O'Connell Bridge**, there are fine views along the river: The Custom House is on the right and to the left is the equally splendid Four Courts. The bridge was built in 1790 and widened until it was almost square in 1880.

Turning left along the quays of the north bank towards the Four Courts (about 1.5 km/1 mile), you will reach the cast-iron **Ha'penny Bridge**, which connects Merchants' Arch to Liffey Street. The footbridge was built in 1816, and its name refers to the toll once levied for crossing. Looking up river from here, you can see the green-topped column of the smock windmill (the largest in Europe) in the Guinness Brewery. Christ Church and the Catholic St Audoen's will also come into view.

On the corner of Liffey Street is a **sculpture** known locally as 'the hags with the bags'. Two doors down from the bridge is the Winding Stair bookshop, which is worth a browse.

The imposing Four Courts building

The Custom House, dominating the north bank of the river

The **Four Courts** was designed by James Gandon in 1785 after the death of the original architect. With its magnificent Corinthian portico crowned with statues and its columned dome, the building is a majestic sight. It holds the various courts of the city, together with a library of law and a basement restaurant. The Four Courts was damaged in the fighting of the 1920s and a terrific fire destroyed all the official archives, but restoration work in 1932 has removed nearly all traces of the destruction. You can step inside when the courts are in session (open: Mon–Fri 9.30am–4pm). At the far end of Inns Quay is the site of the first bridge across the Liffey, built in 1214.

Just beyond the Four Courts, turn north into Church Street, where you'll find the fascinating **St Michan's Church** (tours: Mon–Fri 10am–12.45pm, 2–4.45pm; admission charge). One of the oldest churches in Dublin, it was built in the 17th century on the site of a Danish chapel, but heavily restored in the 19th century. Handel is believed to have practiced on the 1724 organ here while composing *The Messiah*. The church's chief claim to fame, however, is its vaults, which, because of their limestone composition, preserve bodies buried there in a mummified state. A few of the bodies are on display. Robert Emmet is thought to be buried in the graveyard of the church, and Parnell's funeral service was held here. Afterwards, you may well want to drop in at the Old Jameson Distillery in cobbled Bow Street.

The **Old Jameson Distillery** (open: daily 9.30am–6pm, last tour 5.30pm; admission charge) is in Smithfield, the heart of Old Dublin. If you ever wanted to know more about the fascinating craft of whiskey making, this award-winning attraction is the place to find out. Located on the original site of the Jameson Distillery, it also offers a history of the distillery itself. Tours are hosted by multilingual guides.

The **Ceol–Irish Traditional Music Centre** (open: Mon–Sat 9.30am–6pm, Sun noon–6pm; admission charge), in Smithfield Village, explores the relationship of Irish music to Irish history. The exhibits illustrate the important connection between music and Irish culture, and are well worth seeing, as are the live performances.

If you turn right instead of left from O'Connell Bridge, you will come to one of Dublin's great architectural masterpieces, the **Custom House** (Visitor Centre open mid-Mar–mid-Nov: Mon–Fri 10am–5pm, Sat–Sun 2–5pm; winter: Wed–Fri and Sun only). Built in 1791 and designed by James Gandon as his first Dublin masterpiece, it has undergone thorough renovation. It is perhaps best appreciated from the south bank of the river, though more detail can be seen from the closer vantage point on the north bank.

The elegance and grace of this building have something to do with its human dimensions, for although it stands 114m (375ft) high and 61m (200ft) wide, its height does not in the least overwhelm. The sculpture on the dome (a personification of Commerce) and the river gods (including Anna Livia, set over the main door) are by Edward Smyth, who was also responsible for the statues on the GPO *(see page 61)*. The north side of the building has statues by Joseph Banks depicting Africa, America, Asia and Europe.

Statues on O'Connell Street

➤   On Custom House Quay is Dublin's **Famine Memorial**.
Unveiled in 1998, this is a series of striking life-size bronze
figures by sculptor Rowan Gillespie. Their gaunt and emaci-
ated features are given added poignancy by the fact that they
appear to be walking past the gleaming facade of the Allied
Irish Bank, looking east towards the Irish Sea.

O'Connell Street

O'Connell Street is a grand boulevard with a wide central
island, studded with monuments and statues. It runs in a
straight line north from O'Connell Bridge, and the best way
to view it is to walk down the central island, making excursions to the left and right at the zebra crossings.

   The road was largely destroyed in the Rising (*see page
19*), but was restored by the end of the 1920s. At the foot of
the bridge is John Foley's **monument to Daniel O'Connell**,
surrounded by four victory figures and peppered with bullet

> **'The great appear great because we are on our knees' – Jim Larkin**

holes from 1922. The memorial to working-class hero, orator, and socialist **Jim Larkin** by Oisin Kelly is opposite the famous chiming clock (notice the several imitators down the boulevard) of **Clerys**, largest department store in Ireland. Farther up on the right is one of Dublin's legendary hotels, the Gresham, which was built in 1817, seven years before the Shelbourne. The Georgian interior of the ground floor is worth a look.

Perhaps the most memorable monument in Dublin is the **General Post Office** (open: Mon–Sat 8am–8pm) in the centre of O'Connell Street. Built in 1815–18, and one of the last great buildings to come out of Dublin's Georgian boom, the GPO is justly renowned for its imposing Ionic portico (look for the bullet holes) with six fluted columns and figures sculpted by Edward Smyth. It was here, in 1916, that James Connolly and Padraig Pearse barricaded themselves inside and proclaimed the Irish Republic. The post office was virtually destroyed in the fighting but has since been fully restored. The Rising is commemorated in the main hall by a beautiful bronze statue of the mythic folk hero **Cúchulainn** and by ten paintings illustrating various scenes of the rebellion.

Just off Lower O'Connell Street on the corner of Lower Abbey Street and Marlborough Street is the **Abbey Theatre** *(see page 89)*. Founded in 1904 by W.B. Yeats, Lady Augusta Gregory and Edward Martyn, the theatre has long been a showcase for great Irish writing. The early works of Sean O'Casey and John Synge were written for the Abbey. The present Abbey Theatre dates from from 1966, since a fire in 1951 destroyed the original building. It now forms part of the National Theatre, alongside the Peacock Theatre located just around the corner.

Stunning stained glass graces the Chapel of the Rotunda Hospital

Situated just north of the Abbey Theatre and parallel with O'Connell Street in Marlborough Street is the Catholic **St Mary's Pro-Cathedral**, the main Catholic parish church of the city centre, built between 1816 and 1825. Its somewhat forbidding classical Doric exterior seems to dwarf the street (it was designed originally for O'Connell Street). The domed Renaissance interior is in restrained blues and greys, and is curiously unadorned. However, the Palestrina choir that sings Mass on Sundays is excellent, and attracts large numbers of visitors.

Opposite the cathedral is **Tyrone House** (not open to the public), home to the Department of Education. Built in 1742 by Richard Castle, the interior features work by the Francini brothers (also responsible for Newman House). Outside is a gift to the people of Ireland from the Italian government in gratitude for relief supplies during World War II: a marble Pietà entitled *La Deposizione*, by Ermenegildo Luppi.

It is worth making a detour on the pedestrianised areas of **Henry Street** and **Moore Street**, to see their famous markets and hear the cries of the stallholders *(see page 84)*. Expect some ribald remarks in broad Dublin accents. Moore Street Market is open Monday to Saturday and specialises in fruit, vegetable and flowers. This area is quickly becoming the multi-ethnic hub of Dublin's growing immigrant community. Alongside the fruit stalls are shops selling Russian, African and Chinese specialities.

At the northern end of the street is the 1911 **monument to Parnell** by Augustus St-Gaudens. Notice anything odd? Yes, he is wearing two overcoats (apparently he always did).

Parnell Square

Compared to the Georgian squares south of the Liffey, the area around **Parnell Square** looks rather shabby, but once it was just as fashionable and affluent. On the south side of Parnell Square are the **Rotunda Hospital** and the Gate Theatre. The Palladian-style Rotunda was built by Richard Castle in 1751–1755; it's Europe's oldest maternity hospital. The chapel on the first floor, with stained-glass windows and rococo plasterwork, has served at different times as an Assembly Room and a cinema; Charles Dickens also gave readings here. What is now the **Gate Theatre** *(see page 89)* was built in 1784 and is probably the most beautiful stage in Dublin. The theatre company was founded in 1930 by Michael MacLiammóir and Hilton Edwards, and is still going strong today, with an excellent reputation for international and innovative work. James Mason and Orson Welles began their acting careers here. The theatre is now a popular venue for contemporary music concerts.

The **Garden of Remembrance** (open from morning until sunset) on the north side of Parnell Square is dedicated to those who lost their lives in the cause of Irish freedom and features a cruciform lake and Oisin Kelly's beautiful sculpture of the *Children of Lir*.

Across the road from the Garden of Remembrance are two museums, the Hugh Lane Municipal Gallery of Modern Art and the Dublin Writers Museum.

The **Hugh Lane Municipal Gallery of Modern Art** (open: Tues–Thur 9.30am–6pm, Fri–Sat 9.30am–5pm, Sun 11am–5pm, closed Mon; free) occupies a home built for Lord Charlemont by Sir William Chambers. Restored in 1991, this handsome building is worth seeing for itself alone, as well as for the splendid art collection. Sir Hugh Lane, who died in 1915, bequeathed his collection of paintings to the Irish government and the National Gallery in London. The collection includes works by Manet, Degas and other French impressionists as well as their Irish counterparts. The post-impressionist paintings of Jack B. Yeats (brother of the famous poet) are particularly noteworthy. Recent acquisitions include the work of such contemporary artists as Vivienne Roche and Patrick O'Reilly. The building itself is highly interesting, and there is an excellent café in the basement.

Next door, the **Dublin Writers Museum** (open: Mon–Sat 10am–5pm, until 6pm June–Aug, Sun 11am–5pm; admission charge), also restored in 1991, is an intriguing combination of

---

Another Monument to Irish Humour

Plans for the Millennium (construction is progressing on Irish time) include the restoration of O'Connell Street to its former glory. An entertainment centre and shopping mall are projected. However, the much-discussed Millennium Needle, a stainless steel edifice to have been placed in the centre of the street was cancelled (it had already been nicknamed the 'Stiffie by the Liffey' in Dublin pubs).

Dublin's novelists, playwrights and poets are remembered at the Dublin Writers Museum

Georgian exterior and Victorian interior. No one interested in Irish writing and theatre should miss this light and elegant museum covering the long Irish literary tradition, displaying first editions, theatre programmes, correspondence, clothing and other memorabilia. The collection begins with medieval Irish writing and ends with Brendan Behan, Liam O'Flaherty and Sean O'Faoláin. There are frequent exhibitions and events, and the Writers Centre provides a place for talk and work. Upstairs is a portrait gallery. There is a children's room and a bookshop, and a good café and restaurant.

East of Parnell Square, along North Great George's Street, is the **James Joyce Cultural Centre** (open: Mon–Sat 9.30am–5pm, Sun 12.30–5pm; admission charge). This interesting museum and cultural centre is housed in a mansion dating from 1784 and run by Joyce's nephew. The centre contains a library, exhibition rooms, and a study centre devoted to

Home of the President of the Republic in Phoenix Park

the great novelist. There is a full programme of events, including lectures, tours of the house and a walking tour of Joycean North Dublin. Joyce himself must have known the house as the residence of Mr Denis J. Maginni, 'professor of dancing', who appears several times in the novel *Ulysses*.

Phoenix Park

On the banks of the Liffey, just 3km (2 miles) from the bustle of O'Connell Street, lies the biggest urban park in Europe, comprising some 709 hectares (1,750 acres) of landscaped gardens, woods, pastures and playing fields. The park is a graceful and elegant expanse with fine views of the mountains, much loved by Dubliners since it was first opened to the public in 1747. Self-guided heritage walks and several nature trails are marked by black information plaques.

The oldest building in the park is **Ashtown Castle**, a former papal residence which has been renovated to house the splendid **Phoenix Park Visitor Centre** (open: 9.30am–5pm; admission charge; wheelchair access), which presents a video and an excellent two-floor exhibition on the history and wildlife of the park. The castle itself comprises an early 17th-century tower house, restored with Irish oak from the park which is held together without a single nail. Outside there is a young garden maze, marking the outline of the original foundations, and a restful café.

The park also boasts the tallest obelisk in Europe in the 67-m (220-ft) **Wellington Monument**, erected in 1861 after the victory of Waterloo. The Wicklow granite is faced with plaques cast from captured and melted-down cannon. Not quite as large is the **Papal Cross**, commemorating Pope John Paul II's visit in 1979, when more than one million people gathered to celebrate Mass.

The **Phoenix Column**, dating from 1747, stands near the natural spring from which the name of the park is derived (the result of an English corruption of the Gaelic *fionn uisce*, meaning 'clear water').

Occupying more than 12 hectares (30 acres), the **Dublin Zoo** (open summer: Mon–Sat 9.30am–6pm, Sun 10.30am–6pm; winter: Mon–Sat 9.30am–dusk, Sun 10.30am–dusk; admission charge) was founded in 1831, and has greatly improved in recent years; there are plans for a complete renovation. The landscaped grounds (designed by Decimus Burton, who was also responsible for the park lodges) provide a safe home to more than 700 species, including such endangered animals as snow leopards and golden lion tamarinds. The new **Discovery Centre** is worth a visit.

Also within the sprawling grounds of the park are the official residence of the Irish president, which dates from 1751 (guided tours from the Visitor Centre Sat 9.40am and 4.20pm), and the US ambassador's residence, an 18th-century house which was formerly the official residence of the Viceroy's chief secretary (not open to the public).

SuperSaver Card

Some museums are closed on Monday, and opening hours tend to be restricted during the winter months. The national museums have free admission, but the SuperSaver Card, available at any Tourism Centre or participating attraction, will admit you to a number of others at a reduced price with priority entry.

DAY TRIPS SOUTH OF THE CITY

As if the city itself did not provide enough options, the countryside around Dublin offers a wealth of possible excursions and day trips. The DART railway, running north and south to nearby seaside towns and villages, offers a scenic trip along the coast. If you take the DART south, you'll find the best sandy beaches in Dublin. **Dún Laoghaire** is the major port on the east coast. Here, ferries across the Irish Sea leave from two state-of-the-art piers. West of the harbour is the **National Maritime Museum**. The penultimate stop on the DART is **Bray**, a seaside resort with a beach and amusement arcades. There are splendid views from Bray Head of the harbour and the mountains. You can take the DART on to its terminus at **Greystones**, a pretty coastal town, or you can walk there along the coast yourself – a lovely 45-minute jaunt from Bray.

County Wicklow, also to the south of Dublin, rightly deserves its title, 'Garden of Ireland', with some of the most spectacular scenery in the country: rugged mountains, steep,

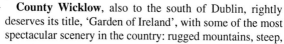

Getting Out

Many bus tours will take you to the various destinations *(see page 114)*, and some are accessible by city bus. Dublin Tourism at Suffolk Street has all the information, and can arrange tours. Car hire is available at the same site *(see page 107)*. It is worthwhile to hire a car so you can go at your own pace. Below are some suggestions for excursions; all can be done in a day or a half day from the city. At the end of each entry in this section is information about how the destination can be reached. Note that some attractions can be seen only by guided tour, and the last admission to these may be 30 to 45 minutes earlier than the official closing time.

wooded river valleys, and deep lakes as well as charming villages and some notable mansions and gardens.

James Joyce Museum

Sandycove, County Dublin.

The **James Joyce Museum** (open Apr–Oct: Mon–Sat 10am–1pm and 2–5pm, Sun 2–6pm; Nov–Mar: by appointment only, tel: 280 9265; admission charge) is one of the most unusual

Interior of the Joyce Museum at the Martello Tower

small museums in or around Dublin. It is housed in a Martello Tower. A series of such towers, some 12m (40ft) high and 2.5m (8ft) thick, were constructed along the coast at the beginning of the 19th century to guard against invasion by Napoleon. Joyce actually lived in the tower very briefly, and it is the location for the first chapter of *Ulysses*. Full of Joycean memorabilia (including his guitar and waistcoat), correspondence, and rare editions of books and manuscripts, it is a shrine for Joyce enthusiasts. DART and bus no. 8.

Avoca and the Avoca Handweavers

Avoca Village, County Wicklow (and Kilmacanogue, Bray).

The picturesque village of **Avoca** became famous as the setting for the BBC TV programme *Ballykissangel*. A company of handweavers has been working here since at least 1723, and visitors are able to watch them as they work; unfortunaely, though, their products are somewhat less distinctive since the place became a popular tourist attraction. There's a shop and a decent café in the small complex of traditional buildings (open: Mon–Fri 9.30am–5.30pm, Sat–Sun 10am–6pm).

Glendalough

County Wicklow.

St Kevin, founder of the monastery at Glendalough, was famed for his patience. One story tells how a bird laid an egg in the palm of his hand; to avoid causing harm, the holy man stayed still until the egg hatched.

The sacred site of **Glendalough** (the name comes from the Irish for 'Valley of the Two Lakes', or Gleann Dá Locha), in the Wicklow Mountains is still highly evocative, and should not be missed. It was the place chosen by St Kevin for a monastery which, over the centuries, became a great spiritual centre of learning, attracting pilgrims from all over Europe. It is set in a beautiful landscape, with clear lakes and streams surrounded by steep wooded hills.

Despite Viking raids, a great fire at the end of the 14th century and long years of neglect, many of the original buildings still stand at Glendalough: the 11th-century round tower (more than 30m/100ft high and 15m/5ft around the base), a 9th-century barrel-vaulted church known as 'St Kevin's Kitchen' and the roofless cathedral. There are also scores of Celtic crosses.

The visitor centre, designed so that it fits into the landscape, provides a 20-minute audiovisual presentation of the history of Irish monasticism, plus an exhibition on the geology and wildlife of the area, and conducts guided tours – but you can also (preferably) wander about on your own. Glendalough's three nature trails take less than an hour's relaxed walking and are well worth doing. The site can be visited by car or bus tour, or by taking St Kevin's bus from the Royal College of Surgeons on St Stephen's Green (leave 11.30am, arrive 1pm, return 4.15pm).

Glendalough is part of the **Wicklow Mountains National Park**, an area of about 200 sq km (78 sq miles), which includes most of upland Wicklow, with spectacular scenery, wildlife and rare flora. The 137-km (85-mile) **Wicklow Way** long-distance footpath wends its peaceful course through the park, much of it above 500m (1,600ft) – bring rain gear and wear sturdy shoes. Call the Education Centre at (0404) 45425 for more information.

Mount Usher Gardens
Ashford, County Wicklow.
The spectacular **Mount Usher Gardens** (open Mar–Oct: daily 10.30am–6pm; admission charge; car or bus tours) were established in 1868 by the Walpole family. The climate and soil are such that plants and trees that would not normally survive this far north are capable of flourishing, which explains the enormous variety of more than 4,000 plants, trees and shrubs from all over the world. The 8-hectare (20-acre) paradise is near Ashford, along the River Vartry. It attracts a range of birds and wildfowl. There is a tearoom on site.

Glendalough is a big draw for tourists

Powerscourt Estate

Enniskerry, County Wicklow.

About 18km (12 miles) from Dublin, outside the pretty village of Enniskerry in the foothills of the Wicklow Mountains, is the **Powerscourt Estate** (open: daily, limited hours in winter; guided tours available; admission charge). It consists of some 5,500 hectares (14,000 acres), hugging the River Dargle. The gardens are among the greatest in Europe, and take in a view of the Sugar Loaf Mountain as part of their design. The enormous Palladian house regrettably was destroyed by fire in 1974. The house now incorporates the restored ballroom, a restaurant overlooking the gardens, an exhibition on the history of the estate, several shops and a garden centre.

The formal splendour of the grounds testifies to the 18th-century desire to tame nature, but it is done with such su-

The grandiose Powerscourt Estate

perlative results that one can only be thankful that the work was undertaken. The broad, sweeping terraces offer magnificent views; statuary rears up out of ornamental lakes; deer roam the parklands; and the Dargle obligingly throws itself over 122m (400ft) of rock to form the highest waterfall in Ireland (4km/2½ miles from the main estate). Children like the pets' cemetery.

Russborough House

Blessington, County Wicklow.

This magnificent Georgian-Palladian house (open for guided tours only May–Sept: daily 10.30am–5.30pm; Apr and Oct: Sun and holidays 10.30am–5.30pm; admission charge), constructed in 1740–1750 and designed by Richard Castle, is one of the earliest Irish great houses. It is constructed on a monumental scale, with a 213-m (700-ft) facade of Wicklow granite, Doric arcades and wonderful ornamentation, all set against an impressive terraced landscape, with the extensive grounds covering some 80 hectares (200 acres).

Irish country houses are generally distinguished by their architecture rather than their contents, but Russborough is a striking exception to this rule. The interiors feature superb plasterwork by the Francini brothers, identifiable, as elsewhere, by their trademark of eagles' heads. The plasterwork on the staircase, with its lavish swags of flowers gently held in the mouths of some very patient-looking dogs is extraordinary. The inlaid floors are particularly lovely, and there are extensive collections of furniture, silver and tapestries.

Also in the house is the impressive **Beit Collection** of paintings, which is shared with the National Gallery; it includes celebrated works by Gainsborough, Goya, Guardi, Hals, Reynolds, Rubens, Velasquez, Vermeer and others, and a series of eight paintings by Murillo depicting the story of the prodigal son.

DAY TRIPS WEST OF THE CITY

Castletown House
Celbridge, County Kildare
When William Connolly, then speaker of the Irish House of
Commons, set his heart on a palatial country home, he
turned to Italian architect Alessandro Galilei, who designed
the facade of the main house in 1722. This Palladian masterpiece, however, was finished by Irishman Edward Lovett
Pearce who is responsible for the colonnades and side pavilions. The result is one of the most graceful and distinctive
houses of the period in Ireland. The house's famous Long
Gallery has Pompeiian fresco-inspired designs and Venetian
chandeliers; the great staircase is the work of Simon Vierpyl;
and the plasterwork is by the Francinis. The grounds (now
sadly encroached upon) are adorned by a a 48-m (140-ft) high
obelisk. (Open late Apr–Sept: Mon–Fri 10am–6pm, Sat–Sun
1–6pm; Oct: Mon–Fri 10am–5pm, Sun 1–5pm; Nov: Sun
1–5pm; admission charge; car or bus 67/67A followed by a
<u>half</u>-mile walk.)

Irish National Stud and Japanese Gardens
Tully, County Kildare.
Horses are immensely popular in Ireland, and County
Kildare can claim to be at the heart of horse country. The
Curragh and Punchestown racecourses are situated here, and
the **Irish National Stud** (open: Feb–Nov daily 9.30am–
6pm; admission charge; combined ticket covers Irish Stud,
Irish Horse Museum, Japanese Gardens and St Fiachras
Garden), home to breeding stallions, has produced some of
the most successful horses in the country. Visitors see horses
being trained and exercised. There is also a museum illustrating the history of the horse in Ireland, which features the
skeleton of the racehorse Arkle.

Adjacent to the stud are the **Japanese Gardens**, created by the stud's founder in the early part of the century, and well worth a visit, and the new **St Fiachras Garden**, created to celebrate the millennium.

DAY TRIPS NORTH OF THE CITY

To the north of Dublin, the DART will take you to the **Howth** peninsula, which affords splendid views along a cliff-top coastal walk. In spring and summer this area is rich in nesting sea birds, as well as interesting land birds and butterflies attracted by the moorland terrain of the cliff top. In July and August there is a wonderful colour combination of purple heather and yellow gorse. Walking up to Howth lighthouse, it is difficult to believe that Dublin is just a few miles away – until you see Dublin Bay spread out before you. Also in Howth is the **National Transport**

County Kildare's Japanese Gardens

Museum (open June–Aug: Mon–Fri 10am–5pm, Sat–Sun 2–5pm; Sept–May: weekends only) at Howth Castle.

National Botanic Gardens
Glasnevin, Dublin 9.
Originally modelled on London's Kew Gardens, Ireland's premier horticultural attraction, the **National Botanic Gardens** (open May–Sept: Mon–Sat 9am–6pm, Sun 11am–6pm; Oct–Apr: Mon–Sat 10am–4.30pm, Sun 11am–4.30pm; glasshouses open at 2pm on Sun; free), was established by the Royal Dublin Society in 1795. With over 20,000 species in more than 20 hectares (50 acres) of grounds, there is plenty to see and enjoy in any season. The four glasshouse groups, built between 1843 and 1868, have been magnificently restored. They include an alpine house, a palm and orchid house, and the Curvilinear Range, a spectacular curving glass-house of cast iron. There are all sorts of different gardens and landscapes, including a riverside walk.

Adjacent to the gardens is the **Glasnevin Cemetery**, where some of the most notable figures in recent Irish history are buried. These include Charles Stewart Parnell, Daniel O'Connell and Éamon de Valera.

Marino Casino
Malahide Road, Dublin 3.
Lord Charlemont's 'marine villa', built in 1762–77, is one of Ireland's finest neoclassical buildings, and certainly one of the most intriguing. Designed by William Chambers (who is responsible for Somerset House in London), it is generally regarded as his masterpiece. It is a building of great ingenuity – from the outside it looks like a small Greek-style temple, but is in fact two storeys high and contains eight rooms. Sculpture and stone carving are perfectly modified to the harmonies of

the design; the four columns at the corners are hollow to carry water off the roof, and the urns on roof are disguised chimneys. The interior has exquisite floors and plasterwork. After years of neglect it was restored, beginning in the mid-1970s, and opened to the public in 1984.

Though it is surrounded by ill-planned encroachments, the Casino still stands in perfect splendour on a gentle rise. Down the road is 'Spite Crescent' built by an enemy of Lord Charlemont to spoil his view from the Casino. It was here that Bram Stoker stayed while writing *Dracula* in 1897.

Malahide Castle
Malahide, County Dublin.

Glasnevin Cemetery

The crenellated **Malahide Castle and Estate** (guided tours only, Nov–Mar: Sat–Sun noon–4pm; Apr: Sat–Sun noon–5pm; May: daily 10am–5pm; June–Sept: daily 10am–6pm; Oct: daily 10am–5pm) in the pretty little seaside town of Malahide (DART station) has been home to the Talbot family for 800 years, and parts of the building date back to the 12th century. Tourists can visit the house, which is a showcase for some of the National Portrait Collection of the National Gallery and also contains fine 18th-century furniture, chinoiserie and children's toys. There are some impressive views of the grounds and distant mountains, particularly from the airy turret rooms.

James Boswell, the biographer of Samuel Johnson, was married to a Talbot, and many of his papers were discovered in the 20th century at the castle. Audio tapes in each room narrate the house's history. There is a craft shop in the grounds, and an excellent restaurant, imaginative café and a bookshop on the ground floor of the castle.

The lush park surrounding Malahide includes the **Talbot Botanic Gardens** (open Apr–Oct: Mon–Sat 10am–5pm, Sun 11am–6pm; Nov–Mar: Mon–Fri 10am–5pm, Sat–Sun 2–5pm; admission charge), 8 hectares (20 acres) of walled gardens and glasshouses with thousands of plant species. Also in the grounds is the **Fry Model Railway Museum** (open late Apr–Sept: Mon–Sat 10am–5pm, Sun 2–6pm; Oct–Nov: daily 1–5pm; admission charge), Ireland's largest O-gauge model railway, with miniature models of trains, railway stations and some of Dublin's landmarks.

Malahide Castle

Newbridge House and Victorian Farm

Donabate, County Dublin.
Newbridge House (open Apr–Sept: Tues–Sat 10am–5pm, Sun 2–6pm; Oct–Mar: weekends only 2–5pm; admission charge) and its es-

tate of some 142 hectares (350 acres) belonged to the Cobbe family from 1736. The beautifully restored house contains some interesting furniture and plasterwork, and there is also a museum of rural life incorporating several artisans' cottages with period furniture and tools.

Newgrange

Slane, County Meath.

Newgrange (open from dawn to dusk; admission charge) is the most important of the prehistoric sites around Dublin, located about 3km (2 miles) east of Slane. It is the best preserved passage tomb in Europe, and is 500 years older than the Pyramids (3000BC). It's a huge mound (nearly 12m/40ft high and almost 90m/300ft wide) and is constructed from 200,000 tons of stone, much of which was somehow hauled from the Wicklow Mountains and the Mountains of Mourne. Newgrange may be the world's oldest solar observatory – the whole edifice is aligned in such a way that for several days of the winter solstice, light from the sun floods the inner chamber for around 17 minutes, a spectacular effect: the guide on the tour attempts to give an idea of this effect by plunging the chamber into darkness and slowly bringing up the light. Visitors who dislike enclosed spaces should be warned that the passage into the barrow is very low and narrow. Newgrange can get very crowded, so try to get there early or take a Bus Éireann tour which secures you privileged access.

Nearby is **Knowth**, an even larger and older complex which dates back to earliest neolithic times. Knowth has two passage graves. The site is still being excavated, and only part of it is open. Guided tours originate from the nearby **Brú na Bóinne Centre** (open June–mid-Sept: daily 9am–7pm; Oct–Apr: 9.30am–5pm; May/late Sept: 9.30am–6.30pm), which has some interesting exhibits.

Tara

County Meath

Tara, situated south of the busy town of Navan, is a familiar name in Celtic myths and legends. The site was the cultural, political and religious centre of early Celtic civilisation and is reputedly where the high kings had their palace. Its importance waned, however, after the arrival of Christianity, and nowadays there's little to see except the hill, the remains of an Iron-Age fort, some pillar stones and the rewarding views over the central Irish plain. In a nearby 19th-century Anglican church is the **visitor centre** (open May–Oct: daily 10am–6pm; admission charge), with exhibits and an audiovisual show. Guided tours are conducted of the site – they begin at the visitors' centre and lead past earthworks and ditches with evocative names such as *Rath na Riogh* (Wall of the Kings) and *Dumha Na nGiall* (Ditch of the Hostages).

The legendary Hill of Tara

WHAT TO DO

Dublin is rapidly becoming a 24-hour city, so there is plenty to enjoy when your sightseeing is done. The city's many pubs are the centre of social life, offering conversation and a quiet pint, food, music and song. There are also lots of late-night clubs. And with first-class shops and a profusion of booksellers, galleries and antiques dealers, you can browse or buy contentedly. If you're feeling active, there are excellent opportunities for sports. For at-a-glance information on the city's entertainment facilities, refer to the map on the cover of this guide.

PUBS

As you walk through Dublin's streets it will sometimes seem that there's a pub on every corner. Pubs are Ireland's living rooms – they provide not only drink and food, but atmosphere, entertainment and amusing talk. You may not fall into conversation in Dublin quite as readily as in a country pub, but you'll find that here, as everywhere, the Irish are welcoming hosts. Most pubs also serve food – they are good places to have lunch – and some have dining rooms. Be warned that the pubs around O'Connell Street can be rough, and at times Temple Bar pubs can be rowdy. Pubs open around 11am and close at 12.30am.

The oldest pub in Dublin is reputedly the Brazen Head (Bridge Street Lower) where, it is claimed, a tavern has stood since the 12th century. Wolfe Tone and his United Irishmen are believed to have

> When you order a Guinness, the bartender fills the glass three quarters and lets it settle before topping it off. Do the same before you take a drink. It should be a smooth, dark black before you tip it back.

met here to plan their rebellion. It's cosy and intimate, with its cobblestone courtyard, and they serve a good pint of Guinness. Other authentic old Dublin pubs include Toner's (Lower Baggot Street), Mulligans (Poolbeg Street), Ryan's (Parkgate Street) and the Long Hall (South Great George's Street) with (reputedly) the city's longest bar counter.

Whatever you are looking for in a pub, Dublin will gladly provide. If you're after traditional music, O'Donoghue's (Merrion Row) and Slattery's (Capel Street) are still among Dublin's best; O'Donoghue's was formerly the haunt of The Dubliners. Jack Nealon's (also in Capel Street) has jazz on Sunday and eclectic music the rest of the week. Mother Redcap's Tavern (Back Lane, off High Street) is a big, relaxed place, also with live music. If you like traditional dancing, go to O'Shea's Merchant (Bridge Street Lower). The Stag's Head (Dame Court) is known for its good food.

Irish pubs are the best place to meet and greet locals

Off Grafton Street is Kehoe's (South Anne Street), a favourite watering hole; and on Duke Street are two pubs with with *Ulysses* connections – Davy Byrne's, where Leopold Bloom ate a gorgonzola sandwich and drank a glass of wine, and Bailey's, a busy, trendy pub on the site of Leopold Bloom's house. Behind the Gaiety Theatre, you'll probably encounter a theatrical crowd in Neary's (Chatham Street). Microbreweries have also appeared in Dublin, and sell their excellent beers at the Dublin Brewing Company (North King Street) and Porterhouse Brewing Company (Parliament Street).

There are many old pubs in Temple Bar, but they are often very tourist-orientated. Oliver St John Gogarty (Fleet Street), named for the man-of-letters who was the model for a character in *Ulysses*, has good traditional and other music and a dining room. There's music upstairs in the small, quaint Ha'penny Bridge Inn (Wellington Quay). The Temple Bar (Temple Bar) attracts a busy, lively crowd; the Norseman (East Essex Street) is favoured by the art crowd, while the Auld Dubliner (Anglesea Street) is a pleasant pub that caters a lot for tourists.

Whether you drink alcohol or not, a trip to Dublin isn't complete without a visit to some of its pubs.

SHOPPING

The main shopping areas are in and around Grafton Street, along Nassau Street, in Temple Bar, O'Connell Street, and Henry Street. Pedestrian Grafton Street is lined with well-known chains such as Marks and Spencer, the Body Shop, HMV records and Laura Ashley, plus the excellent, upmarket Brown Thomas department store. O'Connell Street has more downmarket shops, but two landmarks are still here: Eason's for books and art supplies, and Dublin's largest department store: Clerys, with its famous chiming clock.

Shopping Centres

The three-storey **St Stephen's Green Shopping Centre** is at the top of Grafton Street. Under its glasshouse ceiling you can shop and have a meal at the restaurant under the dome looking out onto the green. It can be very crowded, especially in summer. The **Powerscourt Townhouse** on Clarendon Street (follow the sign from Grafton Street) is more upmarket, and specialises in restaurants and cafés, and antiques, jewellery and designer clothing. Also on Clarendon Street is the smaller **Westbury Mall**, with cafés and fine jewellery shops.

On the other side of Grafton Street, leading into Dawson Street, the **Royal Hibernian Way** is another small shopping mall with some exclusive shops. Dawson Street is lined with bookshops and boutiques. North of the river, the **Jervis Centre** on Henry Street has a selection of shops and department stores, including many UK chains. At the ILAC **Centre**, also on Henry Street (second only to the St Stephen's Green Centre), you'll find numerous clothes shops and a large branch of Dunnes Stores, an Irish clothes- and food-shop chain.

Markets

The oldest is on **Moore Street** (open Mon–Sat). It's famous for the cries of its sellers – the models for Molly Malone of the well-known song. Fruit, vegetables, electronics and a little bit of everything else is on sale here. It's also the place to go to pick up ethnic food and goods.

The pretty **Georges Street Arcade** (open Mon–Sat) is a sheltered market located between Georges and Drury streets. Shops and stalls line this atmospheric little market – a good place for secondhand books, music, vintage clothing and ethnic ware.

The **Temple Bar Food Market** (open Sat) at Meeting House Square turns this touristy centre into the home of speciality foods and gourmet delights. Also on Saturday and Sunday, **Blackrock Market** (on Main Street, near Blackrock DART station) has stalls selling jewellery, designer crafts, books, antiques and clothes. There is a cosy little vegetarian restaurant within the market.

What to Buy

Antiques: There are antiques fairs in Newman House on St Stephen's Green South every second Sunday all year. And don't miss a stroll down Francis Street, Dublin's 'antiques highway', lined with antiques and art stores. Also check out the lovely antiques shops on the second floor of Powerscourt Townhouse.

Art: For contemporary art, especially the work of Irish artists, you should try the Kerlin Gallery (off South Anne Street), the Taylor Galleries (Kildare Street), or the Solomon Gallery (Powerscourt Townhouse). The Temple Bar Gallery (Temple Bar) exhibits the work of up to 40 resident artists and the Apollo Art Gallery on Dawson Street has an equally impressive, if more dishevelled collection for sale.

Fresh produce at market

Books: Eason's on O'Connell Street, is a huge shop with mainstream books, magazines, newspapers, and art-supplies. Waterstone's and Hodges Figgis (of

Warming Irish knitwear

Ulysses fame) are across the street from each other in Dawson Street. Both carry an excellent selection of literature, general books, books on Ireland, and the works of Irish writers. International Books in South Frederick Street specialises in languages. For antiquarian books, go to Cathach Books in Duke Street. In Temple Bar, the bookshop at the Gallery of Photography carries a large selection of photographic publications. The labyrinthine Winding Stair on Ormond Quay is an interesting secondhand bookshop with a café.

Chocolates: Delicious Irish handmade chocolates are on sale at Butler's Irish Chocolates in Grafton Street.

Crafts: The most distinguished place for modern Irish crafts and jewellery is Design Yard on Essex Street in Temple Bar – everything here is of high quality. But the Irish Celtic Craftshop and Which Craft Gallery on Lord Edward Street provide stiff competition. For traditional crafts, the House of Ireland, on the corner of Nassau and Dawson streets carries a fine selection of jewellery, crystal and knitwear. The Tower Craft Design Centre on Pearse Street, off Grand Canal Quay, has a range of crafts made and sold on the premises.

Crystal: Ireland has long been known for its crystal, with famous brands including Waterford Crystal, Cavan, Galway,

Tipperary and Tyrone Crystal. Prices do not vary. Try the House of Ireland *(see page 86)*, or the Tipperary Lifeware on Dawson Street.

Family Crests: There is a vast number of shops specialising in coats of arms on everything from plaques to keychains. Try Heraldic Arts and House of Names, both on Nassau Street.

Food: The Irish supermarket chain, Dunnes Stores (outlets on Middle Abbey Street, St Stephen's Green Shopping Centre, the ILAC Centre) sells Irish smoked salmon: ask for the wild, not farmed, variety. For Irish country cheeses, go to Sheridan's Cheesemongers on South Anne Street, or the Big Cheese Company of Trinity Street.

Knitwear: There are two kinds of knits for sale: expensive traditional handknit sweaters and sweaters 'handknit' on a machine. For the former, go to the House of Ireland on Nassau Street. For the latter, bargains can be found at Blarney Woollen Mills (Nassau Street) and Dublin Woollen Mills (Lower Ormond Quay). The Kilkenny Shop on Nassau street carries a large variety of knitwear and handwoven goods. An Táin (Temple Bar Square) has stylish handknits. Monaghan's (Grafton Arcade) specialises in cashmere.

Linens: Brown Thomas has a great linen department. On the south end of Dawson Street is Needlecraft, specialising in fine Irish linens.

Music: If you're looking for indigenous music, Celtic Note (Nassau Street) and Claddagh Records (Temple Bar) carry a good selection of traditional Irish and other Irish recordings. You can't miss HMV on Grafton Street.

Glittering Waterford Crystal

Photography: If you're looking for basic film and batteries any of the following should be of help: City Cameras on Dawson Street, One Hour Photo on St Stephens Green North, or the Camera Centre on Grafton Street. Spectra Photo near Bewley's on Grafton beat them all to the punch with a 45-minute service. For used equipment, try the Dublin Camera Exchange on Trinity Street.

Pottery and Porcelain: In Nassau Street the Kilkenny Shop has a fine selection.

Souvenirs: Shopping for souvenirs should be an easy task in Dublin. Nassau Street is the best destination for souvenir shops on the quick. Some shops may not be too original, but they have all the trinkets folk back home will be happy to get their hands on. If you have more time, there are some excellent shops spread throughout the city showcasing Irish crafts and design.

Inexpensive souvenirs of a stay in Dublin

Wine: Vaughan Johnson's Fine Wine Shop and Mitchell and Sons on Kildare Street provide a tasty alternative to the world of Guinness and whiskey.

VAT Refunds

Non-EU nationals are entitled to a refund of the Value Added Tax (VAT) charged on items that are purchased to be taken out of the country. Ask the shop for a validated receipt; the Cashback desk at the Dublin Airport will give you an instant refund as you depart. Some tourist-orientated shops take the VAT off credit-card purchases before they charge you. In that case, Customs must stamp the receipt, and you must return it to the shop by mail upon arriving home. Purchases shipped directly from the shop to a non-EU country are not subject to VAT (though you may incur import taxes). If you are travelling on to another EU country, you should collect your VAT refunds at your final point of departure for home.

ENTERTAINMENT

Theatre

Dublin has a proud tradition in theatre which is still very much alive, so advance booking is advisable. The **Abbey Theatre** in Lower Abbey Street is Ireland's national theatre (*see also page 91*). Once on the cutting edge, today its more experimental repertoire is presented on its second, basement stage, the intimate **Peacock**. The **Gate Theatre** in Parnell Square, has a similar tradition, and stages a cosmopolitan mix of Irish and international theatre plus musical acts. It's known for showcasing important new Irish playwrights. In both theatres you'll find the very highest standards of acting and production.

The Victorian **Olympia** in Dame Street is the venue for all sorts of popular theatre, concerts and variety shows. The

W.B. Yeat's epitaph, Drumcliff

Gaiety Theatre in South King Street is worth visiting for its ornate décor alone. It runs a range of productions from plays to variety acts.

For cutting edge theatre, the **Project Arts Centre** in East Essex Street has a lively programme of dance, drama, and performance arts, while **Andrew's Lane** also puts on modern productions. The **Samuel Beckett Theatre** at Trinity College is mainly for drama students, but the standard can be high and it brings some interesting shows in from outside.

Other theatres of note include the **Civic Theatre**, with its broad repertoire of music, drama and comedy productions; the **Point** theatre, a large venue that puts on limited runs of big, Broadway-type productions, comedy and high profile concerts; and the **Crypt Arts Centre** at Dublin Castle, which produces smaller pieces in the crypt of the Chapel Royal. The **Lambert Puppet Theatre** in Monkstown is popular with children.

The most important event of the theatre season is the **Dublin Theatre Festival**, held in October of each year. The festival is a showcase both for high quality international productions and for new Irish plays trying to break into the circuit. A fringe festival precedes this event annually.

Comedy

The International Bar on Wicklow Street has given the start to many famous Irish comedians and is still going strong.

The tradition is just beginning at the Laughter Lounge on Middle Abbey Street, but all the signs are good.

Classical Music and Opera

If you are in search of a romantic evening of live classical music, seek out the National Symphony Orchestra, which can be heard in a year-round programme of concerts at the **National Concert Hall** (NCH) in Earlsfort Terrace. The NCH also hosts jazz and traditional music evenings. Chamber

---

Ireland's National Theatre

Dublin's first theatre opened in 1637, and thereafter the city produced many notable playwrights, including Sheridan, Goldsmith, Wilde and Shaw, but there was nothing particularly 'Irish' about their work. W. B. Yeats wanted to create a distinctly Irish theatre of poetic drama, and he turned for inspiration to the legends of ancient Ireland. He looked for a backer, and found Lady Augusta Gregory, who became his partner. Their first productions were done on a shoestring, wherever they could find a space. Finally, in 1904, they acquired a theatre of their own, and the Abbey was born.

The Abbey's career was not without controversy. J. M. Synge's play, *The Playboy of the Western World*, now recognised as a masterpiece, provoked a riot when it was first staged. Later on, *The Plough and the Stars*, by the Abbey's first great realist playwright, Sean O'Casey, caused similar public outrage, and the police were called to protect the theatre.

After Yeats's death in 1939, the Abbey entered a period of limbo, although its acting tradition continued to be world renowned. Things turned around with the opening of its new theatre in 1966 and the emergence of new Irish playwrights – Brian Friel, Connor McPherson, and Frank McGuinness among others. Today, the Abbey continues its tradition of commitment to new work by Irish authors in both English and Gaelic.

music concerts and recitals are given at the **Irish Museum of Modern Art** at the beautiful Royal Hospital building in Kilmainham. **St Anne's Church** on Dawson Street has lunchtime concerts and the **Bank of Ireland Arts Centre** in Foster Place off College Green has lunchtime and evening concert series. A new venue for classical music is the huge **Helix** complex, at the Dublin City University campus on Collins Avenue. Dublin also has a number of music festivals (*see* Calendar of Events *on page 97*).

Opera Ireland (formerly the Dublin Grand Opera Society) offers short spring and winter seasons based on the standard repertoire at the **Gaiety Theatre** in King Street. The **Lyric** company have several productions a year, involving international artists at various venues. The small but enterprising

Traditional Music

The word *seisiún* – meaning an impromptu evening of music and song, usually in a pub – has a particular resonance for the Irish, and there is plenty of opportunity in Dublin to enjoy traditional Irish sounds. A *seisiún* may start when someone – probably the innocent-looking man sitting in the corner huddled over a pint of Guinness – produces a guitar as if from nowhere, and his neighbour responds by bringing out a well-concealed *bodhrán* (goatskin traditional Irish drum). Soon everyone is joining in.

The mainstay of traditional music is the fiddle. The guitar is something of a latecomer, having arrived around the 1960s, but now it's well established. Other instruments you may hear are the uillean pipes (softer than the Scottish bagpipe), the six-hole wooden flute, the tin whistle, the accordion and the banjo, a transfer from America in the 19th century.

While the real centre of traditional music is in the west, you'll find it played in pubs across Dublin; watch for listings or signs in the pubs.

Opera Theatre Company does two or three performances a year of short operas by contemporary Irish or baroque composers.

Rock, Folk and Jazz

One of Dublin's largest venues is the Point, East Link Bridge, which hosts major pop and rock acts (the smash hit *Riverdance* was staged here). The RDS

Irish flautist

in Ballsbridge also occasionally holds huge open-air concerts. The *Irish Times* carries listings for all such events, and *In Dublin* has up-to-the-minute information. Some of the best music is heard at the mid-size venues: the **Olympia Theatre**, the **Ambassador** (O'Connell Street) and the **Temple Bar Music Centre** in Curved Street, where you can hear everything from local acts to international artists. **Whelans** on Wexford Street is a good place to hear up-and-coming artists.

Dance

Dublin has a number of modern dance and ballet companies that perform at various venues. For traditional Irish dancing, go to **O'Shea's Merchant** (*see* 'Pubs'). **Cultúrlann na hÉireann** holds a *céilí* (an evening of traditional dance) on Friday nights in Monkstown (tel: 280 0295).

Film

O'Connell Street is the main city centre location for the big new-release cinemas, including the historical **Savoy Cinema**. Art-house and international films are shown at the **Irish**

The Temple Bar area is the hub of Dublin's nightlife

Film Centre in Eustace Street. The centre contains the National Film Archive, an information centre, a bookshop and a library. Its two cinemas present a varied programme of new international and archival films. The **Screen** in D'Olier Street also shows international films. In summer, open-air movies are screened in Meeting House Square in Temple Bar.

Nightclubs

As in every other city, nightclubs quickly come and go, so it is essential to check the listings in local publications like *In Dublin* or *Events*.

Quite a few clubs can be found along Leeson Street, although some say 'the strip' has faded a bit in recent years. In Temple Bar, look for **Club M** in Bloom's Hotel in Anglesea Street, and **Bob's Bar** in East Essex Street; the **Kitchen** in the basement of the Clarence Hotel is owned by Bono and the Edge of U2. **Ri Ra**, a friendly club located in Dame

Street, is popular with students. **Henry's**, at the Henry Grattan lounge in Baggot Street, serves good food.

Busloads flock nightly to hear middle-of-the-road Irish cabaret at Jury's Hotel in Ballsbridge and Doyle's Irish Cabaret in the Burlington Hotel in Leeson Street.

SPORTS

Golf
Golf is very popular, and there are many superb courses in and around Dublin. The Royal Golf Club at Dollymount and many other clubs welcome visitors; booking is rarely required. Contact Dublin Tourism or the **Golfing Union of Ireland** (tel: 269 4111) for information.

Fishing
Sea angling is permitted all year, but river fishing requires a licence. Information can be obtained from Dublin Tourism or any fishing shop.

Spectator Sports
The traditional Irish games of **hurling** and **Gaelic football** are played at Croke Park. **Horse racing** takes place at Leopardstown; and at the Curragh, (flat racing) and Punchestown, (National Hunt racing) in County Kildare. The premiere **show jumping** event is the Kerrygold Horse Show at the RDS. **Greyhound racing** is on at Shelbourne Park,

Fishing: a popular Irish pastime

A popular children's attraction

Ringsend, and at Harold's Cross Stadium. **Rugby** and **football** (soccer) are played at Lansdowne Road in Ballsbridge.

Watersports/Beaches

There are beaches at Malahide and Dollymount, but the best ones are in the south, at Bray and Killiney. At Sandycove there's the **Forty Foot** bathing spot, once a men's nude beach, but now open to everyone. It is not advisable to swim within 8km (5 miles) of the city centre because of pollution.

DUBLIN FOR CHILDREN

There are plenty of things for children to enjoy in Dublin. Note that family tickets are available for rail and bus services and that children under 16 travel at half-fare on buses and DART.

The Ark, on Eustace Street in Temple Bar, is a children's cultural centre that offers a changing programme of plays, workshops, readings and performances, all geared towards youngsters. It's best to book in advance for the activities, as The Ark has become quite popular, and activities sometimes fill up in advance (tel: 670 7788). The well-loved **Lambert Puppet Theatre** in Monkstown stages panto-style plays geared for young audiences.

Museums that will appeal to children include the **Fry Model Railway Museum** *(see page 78)* at Malahide Castle and Estate *(see page 77)*, while the **National Wax Museum**

(Granby Row, Dublin 1; tel: 872 6340) has a special 'Children's World' tableau depicting well-known fairytale characters and a Hall of the Megastars devoted to pop musicians.

There are nature trails in **Phoenix Park** and the **Dublin Zoo** has a pet corner and zoo train especially designed for younger children *(see page 67)*.

Older children should enjoy **Dublinia** *(see page 43)*, a lively re-creation of medieval 'Diflin', while the self-guided **Rock 'n' Stroll Trail** around Dublin, which follows in the footsteps of Irish rock legends, should appeal particularly to the teenage crowd.

Calendar of Events

February/March Rugby Six Natons Championships: Landsdowne Road, Ballsbridge.

March St Patrick's Day Parade: marching bands from all over the world and live music in a festive atmostphere.

Guinness Temple Bar Fleadh: traditional music festival, indoor and outdoor concerts and traditional dancing, Temple Bar area.

April Dublin Film Festival: films, seminars and lectures at various cinema venues.

June Bloomsday: Dublin city centre. Celebration of Joyce and *Ulysses* in city streets and parks, and at the Joyce Museum, Sandycove.

July Guinness Blues Festival: live music in venues and bars all over Dublin city centre.

August Kerrygold Horse Show: RDS, Ballsbridge. International equestrian event. Dún Laoghaire Festival: parades, music, sports events.

September All-Ireland Hurling and Football Finals: Croke Park.

Irish Antique Dealers Fair: Ballsbridge. International antiques fair.

October Dublin Theatre Festival: Abbey and Gate theatres and other venues. Companies from all over the world, plus new Irish work.

December National Crafts Fair of Ireland: RDS, Ballsbridge.

EATING OUT

The days of overcooked cabbage, mountains of boiled potatoes, and cholesterol-laden fried meat are long gone in Dublin. Not only is there a new Irish cuisine, created by imaginative young chefs, but ethnic restaurants of all kinds give a wider choice than ever before.

Of course, Dublin has always had the fresh ingredients for a fine cuisine. Situated as it is on the broad sweep of Dublin Bay, with the waters of the Atlantic nearby and a plethora of streams and rivers, the city has access to both sea and freshwater fish in abundance – succulent oysters, freshly caught lobster and crab, wild salmon, sole and pike. Tender lamb comes from Kerry and Wicklow; country cheeses, made on farms and in monasteries have begun to achieve a worldwide reputation. Irish breads, apple tarts and fruit cakes have always been delicious, and are still here. So are traditional Irish dishes, but prepared with greater delicacy and lightness of touch. And there are restaurants that cater for vegetarians.

Meals and Meal Times

Breakfast is either the 'continental' variety – fruit juice, rolls, coffee or tea – or traditional Irish, which generally means robust portions of fried eggs, bacon, tomatoes and sausages, black pudding and bread, washed down with coffee or strong tea. Most hotels and restaurants serve breakfast from around 6 or 7am until about 10am.

Lunch is from around noon until 2.30 or 3pm, with the busiest time from 1 to 2pm. Many of the more expensive restaurants offer three- or four-course set lunches, but you can also find simple salads, sandwiches or hot meals at most pubs, cafés and snack-bars. Pubs are often crowded at lunchtime, especially in the city centre. Most cafés serve snacks and light meals all day from 8.30 or 9am until 6pm, though many stay open until as late as 1 or 2am.

Shellfish is very popular

Dinner hours usually begin around 6pm. Many restaurants offer an early pre-theatre dinner that's usually a good bargain. Fixed-price meals are often the best value. Some restaurants open for evening meals only. If you want to dine at the most popular hours – from around 7.30 to 8.30pm – you should book ahead; booking is mandatory at famous or expensive restaurants. It's also worth remembering that VAT on wine adds considerably to the final bill.

Where to Eat

The choice in Dublin ranges from elegant restaurants, often with French or Modern Irish cuisine, to the humble chip shop offering crispy batter-coated portions of tasty fish and chips (try the famous Leo Burdock's at 2 Werburgh Street, near the Castle and Christ Church Cathedral). In between, there are pubs, bistros and moderately priced restaurants of all kinds. Dublin's restaurants range from those serving traditional dishes to Chinese, Creole, Indian, Indonesian, Japanese, Thai, vegetarian cuisine and more.

There are also cafés, self-service snack bars, and the usual fast-food places. Standards of service can vary considerably from one place to the next, but most establishments are welcoming and friendly. Pubs are a good choice for lunch, and often have dining rooms where you can have dinner. For our selection of places to eat, turn to page 135.

Important for the visitor are the often superior cafés and restaurants in the many museums, great houses, and at other attractions. They offer everything from pastries and snacks to hot meals with wine. One of the most delightful cafés is to be found in the Irish Film Centre, located in the trendy Temple Bar district. Another excellent café-restaurant is at the Irish Museum of Modern Art, in the recently opened Millennium Wing, while the National Gallery museum café (an outlet of Fitzer's) is also good – and stays open until 8pm on Thursday.

Cafés and Tearooms

While Dublin's abandonment of tea in favour of coffee is wholesale, the Dublin traditional high tea is still going strong in the city's grand hotels like the Shelbourne and the Gresham. To the background strains of soothing Irish harp or piano music, a liveried waiter will bring you a pot of freshly brewed tea and a silver tray laden with dainty sandwiches, scones, sweet cakes and pastries.

Dublin's lively coffee scene

Dublin is full of cafés where you can get an excellent cup of coffee (and tea if you must) along with a pastry, or a more substantial meal. Cafés also provide the best places to sit and watch the world rush by. Gloria Jean's, on South William Street, serves a formidable cup of coffee. There are plenty of delicatessens and sandwich bars that cater for the quick-business lunch trade, and many of these are very good indeed.

WHAT TO EAT

Starters and Main Courses

It's no surprise that **fish** and **seafood** figure largely on Dublin menus. Wild Irish salmon tops the list. It can be poached or steamed and served simply with a wedge of lemon. Alternatively, it can be smoked over oak branches, thinly sliced, and finely dressed with capers.

Dublin Bay prawns are also very popular as a starter . However you choose to eat them, they are always plump, juicy and delicious. Galway Bay oysters are scrumptious – best with a pint of Guinness. A variety of freshwater fish, mussels from Wexford (try the mussel soup), Donegal crab and Dingle Bay lobster complete the list.

The traditional roast leg of **lamb** can be transformed with black olives and garlic; stuffed fillet of lamb with apple and mint sauce; rack of lamb persillade (with chopped parsley) with courgettes... the list is endless. Irish **beef** comes in a variety of guises, and the prevailing culinary climate has produced such delicacies as beef stuffed with oysters, stir-fried beef with ginger, fillets of beef with cream cheese and mushrooms, and, as you might expect, beef cooked in Guinness or Irish whiskey.

Ham and **pork** also feature strongly on Irish menus, from tender Limerick ham to those plump sausages that serve as an accompaniment to salty home-cured bacon on the Irish breakfast table. Home-raised, free-range chicken is full of flavour. It may be served roasted, wrapped with bacon or ham and stuffed with a savoury herb filling, or more exotically, as chicken breast wrapped around a salmon or walnut mousse.

Traditional Irish dishes have not escaped the effects of nouvelle cuisine. Many restaurants have given old recipies a new twist. Some old-fashioned dishes to look for include *colcannon* (mashed potatoes with leeks and cabbage), *crubeens* (pigs' trotters), *coddle* (boiled bacon, sausages, onions and potatoes), *boxty* (a tasty potato pancake filled with meat, vegetables or fish), Dublin Lawyer (lobster, flamed in whiskey and simmered in cream) and, of course, the traditional Irish stew, made with lamb, potatoes and vegetables.

Vegetarians are particularly well catered for in Dublin. There are quite a few specialist and semi-specialist vegetarian places, and often you'll have a choice between dishes like vegetable couscous, or parsnips stuffed with brazil nuts and vegetables in a red pepper sauce or the unspectacular, though equally delicious, tagliatelle with mushrooms and tomatoes – the many Italian restaurants are always good for vegetarian options. Cornupcopia on Wicklow Street is strictly vegetarian and serves such a variety of tasty of daily specials, you may decide not to eat anywhere else while in the capital.

Bread, Pastries and Desserts

You could find wonderful freshly baked Irish breads even in the old boiled-potato days. Unfortunately, the pseudo-croissant is now ubiquitous, but happily so are soda bread, wholemeal bread, and all manner of scrumptious scones. Old-fashioned classic Irish confections like porter cake and barmbrack are also still around.

Whatever your choice of dessert, you will usually be asked if you want cream with it. Irish cream is thick and delicious, particularly when served with apple tart. Dessert cakes, puddings, and ice-cream dessert combinations tend to be sweet and rich, so be prepared for a major test of your dietary resolve.

Drinks

Dublin wouldn't be Dublin without the world-famous stout, Guinness, which really does taste better here than anywhere else. The pouring and settling process takes a little time, but it's worth the wait. Murphy's and other Irish stouts are also wonderful. Don't miss the range of brews now available from microbreweries.

There is also a great array of distinctive Irish whiskeys – you'll see their names etched in the glass of pub windows. Wine is readily available everywhere, with a fine selection of Australian cabernets and chardonnays, and Chilean wines. Light Italian reds also feature prominently on wine lists. The cheapest way to order wine is to ask for a carafe of the house wine with your meal. Remember that VAT is charged on wine. It's generally cheaper in Dublin to drink in pubs rather than hotel bars. Prices are highest in the city centre.

A pleasure worth waiting for

HANDY TRAVEL TIPS

An A–Z Summary of Practical Information

A

ACCOMMODATION (See also YOUTH HOSTELS and the selection of RECOMMENDED HOTELS starting on page 127)

Hotels in Ireland are classified by star ratings from one to five stars, and are registered and regularly inspected by the Irish Tourist Board (Bord Fáilte). The Tourist Board also publishes a list of approved hotel and guesthouse accommodation throughout Dublin, obtainable through your local tourist information office (for addresses and phone numbers, see Tourist Information). Hotel information can also be found on the Irish Hotels Federation website <www.beourguest.ie>.

All tourism information offices operate an accommodation reservation service, for which a small charge is made. It is always advisable to book accommodation in advance, especially if you plan to visit in the peak months of July and August.

Hotels generally offer a full range of services, including restaurants, licensed bars, currency exchange offices, gift shops and lounges, while **guesthouses** provide more limited facilities, but are excellent value. Be aware that room prices quoted normally include the government tax (VAT) of 12.5 percent but do not always include service charges, which will add an extra 10 to 15 percent to your bill. Breakfast is often extra. Ask when you book. If a room is referred to as 'en suite', it means that the room has a private bath.

Details about **self-catering accommodation** in Dublin and the surrounding area can be obtained from the Irish Tourist Board (which produces a complete illustrated guide). Dublin also offers a variety of college and **university accommodation** when classes are not being held. Rooms and apartments at bargain rates are available on the Trinity College campus between June and September. For further information, contact the Accommodation Office, Trinity College, Dublin 2; tel: 608 1177; fax: 671 1267; <www.tcd.ie>. University College Dublin provides a similar service. For further information, contact UCD Village, Belfield, Dublin 4; tel: 269 7111; fax: 269 7704;

<www.ucd.ie>. Details of student accommodation can be obtained from the Irish Student Travel Service, 19 Aston Quay, Dublin 2; tel: 679 8833.

Holiday Hostels provide simple accommodation in dormitory-style rooms or shared bedrooms for visitors on a tight budget and are open all year. For details of hostels in Dublin, contact the Irish Tourist Board. Three places you can contact directly are:

Avalon House, Budget Accommodation Centre, 55 Aungier Street, Dublin 2; tel: 475 0001; fax: 475 0303; <www.avalon-house.ie>.

Kinlay House Dublin, Accommodation Centre, 2–12 Lord Edward Street, Dublin 2; tel: 679 6644; fax: 679 7437.

Bedfinders on O'Connell Street near the GPO; tel: 878 3949.

AIRPORTS

Dublin International Airport is about 11km (7 miles) north of the city centre. A moderately sized modern complex, it offers a range of facilities, including a duty-free shopping centre, tourism information office, bank, bureau de change, post office, and branches of the major car hire firms. The airport is managed by Aer Rianta (information line tel: 814 4222).

The airport is serviced by bus and taxi. **Airlink**, a regular shuttle service connecting it to the city centre is operated by Dublin Bus <www.dublinbus.ie>. Buses leave from outside the Arrivals Hall and connect with the central bus station (Busáras), railway stations (Heuston Station, Connolly Rail/DART station) and the city centre. Buses leave every ten minutes from 5.45am until 11pm; buy tickets from the bus driver. **Aircoach** <www.aircoach.ie> operates a competing 24-hour service with buses leaving every 15 minutes from 5am–midnight and hourly after that. A cheaper option, if you have plenty of time, is to take city buses 41, 41A, 41B or 41C to the city centre. An **Air DART** bus takes people the short way to Howth Junction DART Station. From there you can access any station on the DART network. Taxis line up outside the Arrivals Terminal.

C

CAR HIRE/RENTAL (See also DRIVING)

It is worth hiring a car to explore the countryside around Dublin, although driving a car in the heavy city traffic is not advisable. You can arrange to hire a car immediately upon arrival at Dublin airport, or have one waiting for you if you book a fly-drive or rail-sail-drive inclusive package. Major car hire companies are represented at the airport, and there are many local firms listed in the Golden Pages of the telephone directory.

To hire a car you'll need a driving licence issued in your home country, valid for at least two to five years. The minimum age (usually 23–26 years) varies from company to company. Rates include third-party liability insurance, but collision damage waiver (CDW) must be paid for separately at about €10 per day. Personal accident insurance (PAI), theft insurance, and third party property damage (TPPD – without it the hirer will typically be responsible for the first €1,500 of damage) are also available, each costing about €5 per day. There's also a charge for an extra driver. Road assistance is supplied by the Automobile Association (23 Suffolk Street, Dublin 2; Emergency Service; tel: 677 9481).

Major car hire companies.

Avis, Airport Arrivals Hall and 1E Hanover Street, Dublin 2; tel: 605 7555; <www.avis.ie>.

Budget, Airport Arrivals Hall and 151 Drumcondra Road Lower, Dublin 9; tel: 837 9611; <www.budgetcarrental.ie>.

Hertz, Airport Arrivals Hall and 149 Leeson Street Upper, Dublin 4; tel: 660 2255; <www.hertz.com>.

National, Airport Arrivals Hall and Cranford Centre, Stillorgan, Dublin 4; tel: 260 3771; <www.carhire.ie>.

Argus, a local company, is at the Dublin Tourism Centre, Suffolk Street, Dublin 2; tel: 490 4444; <www.argus-rentacar.com>.

CLIMATE

Dublin's climate is temperate, without extremes of temperature, thanks to the warming Gulf Stream that influences much of the country. Contrary to popular belief, rain is not a permanent condition, but – due to blustery winds coming in from the Irish Sea – the weather is unpredictable and can change very quickly from rain to sun (and vice versa). Less rain falls on Dublin than on any other part of the country, however, and snow is a rare occurrence. Summers can be quite cool, and days can be unexpectedly warm in winter.

	J	F	M	A	M	J	J	A	S	O	N	D
°C	7	8	11	13	16	18	20	21	17	14	11	8
°F	45	46	52	55	61	64	68	70	63	57	52	46

CLOTHING

Dubliners are fashion-conscious, and a certain standard of attire is expected in exclusive hotels and restaurants. Business people still dress in formal dark suits. For everyday wear, however, jeans and casual clothes are appropriate. A raincoat or umbrella are absolute necessities. If you plan to walk a lot, especially in the environs, bring sturdy shoes and a sweater: even if it looks like a glorious day, it can turn cold later on. Pack warm clothing for winter, and a jacket and sweater in summer. Evening temperatures on the sunniest summer days can be quite cool, and in spring there is often a chilling wind, which adds an edge to the day's mild warmth.

CRIME AND SAFETY (See also EMERGENCIES)

Compared to most urban centres, Dublin's crime rate is moderate, and violent street crime is rare. However, crime is unfortunately on the upswing. Take sensible measures. Leave your valuables in the hotel safe, keep your wallet in an inside pocket or hang your bag strap across your chest. Be wary of pickpockets in pubs or crowded places, and don't flash your money around when using street side ATMs. Don't leave objects unattended or open to view in a parked car. At night stay where the crowds are, walk with confidence, and sit near the bus driver if you are travelling to a suburb.

If you are robbed, report the incident to the hotel receptionist and the nearest police station, so that the police can provide you with a certificate to present to your insurance company. Call your consulate if your passport has been stolen. Tourist information offices and some attractions provide a multilingual leaflet produced by the Gardai (see also Police), entitled *A Short Guide to Tourist Security*.

CUSTOMS AND ENTRY REQUIREMENTS

For a stay of up to three months in Ireland, a valid passport is sufficient for citizens of Australia, Canada, New Zealand, South Africa and the US. Visitors from European Union (EU) countries need only bring an identity card and are free to stay indefinitely in the country, and work if they wish.

Since Ireland is a member of the EU, free exchange of non-duty-free goods for personal use is permitted between Ireland and the continent. If you are from a non-EU country, you are still entitled to a duty-free allowance: 200 cigarettes, 50 cigars or 250g tobacco; 2 litres of wine and 1 litre of spirits; and 60ml perfume. Meat, meat products, vegetables, fruit and the like may not be brought into Ireland. Porno graphic materials are also prohibited. There are no currency restrictions.

For residents of non-EU countries returning home, the allowances are: Australia: A$400 of goods, 250 cigarettes or 250g tobacco or 100 cigars; 1 litre spirits or wine; Canada: $500 of goods, 200 cigarettes and 50 cigars; 1 litre spirits or wine or 8.5 litres beer; New Zealand: NZ$700 of goods, 250g of tobacco products; 4.5 litres wine or beer and 1 litre spirits; South Africa: 400 cigarettes and 50 cigars and 250g tobacco; 2 litres wine and 1 litre spirits; US: $400 of goods, 200 cigarettes and 100 non-Cuban cigars or 2kg tobacco, 1 litre wine or spirits; antiques over 100 years old are also allowed.

D

DRIVING

Road Conditions. Rush-hour traffic jams and limited parking space make driving in central Dublin an unpleasant experience. Bottlenecks form rapidly on the city's narrow streets, especially in rush hours. If you must drive in the city centre, try and plan your journey between 10am and 4pm to avoid the worst congestion.

Outside the city is a motorway system for rapid transit, but most scenic routes, such as those through the Wicklow Mountains, tend to be narrow, winding and steep, with bad visibility and possible ice in winter. Road users in Ireland tend to take everyone's life in their hands: speeding and overtaking at heartstopping places – drive defensively.

Rules and Regulations. Traffic follows the same basic rules that apply in Britain. Drive on the left, pass on the right. Turn left on a roundabout (traffic circle); at a junction where no road has priority, yield to traffic coming from the right. Road signs giving place directions are bilingual, in Irish and English, and distances are shown in kilometres. Seat belts in both the front and back must be worn, and children under 12 must travel in the rear. Ireland has very strict rules about drinking and driving – don't do it.

Petrol (gas). There are filling stations everywhere, many of them are self-service. A number are open 24 hours. Petrol is sold by the litre and comes in three grades: lead replacement petrol, unleaded and super unleaded.

Parking. It's almost impossible to find free parking on Dublin's streets during normal working hours, but you may have better luck at week-ends. Expect to be towed away or heavily fined for parking illegally. Metered parking (for up to 2 hours) is quite limited. Your safest bet is to park in one of the multistorey car parks, which are not expensive: around €1.50 an hour, with a flat evening rate. Look for computerised signs giving information about availability.

Speed limits. The speed limit is 96 km/h (60 mph) on open roads and 112 km/h (70 mph) on motorways. In built up areas, speed is restricted to 48 km/h (30 mph). Cars towing trailers may not exceed 80 km/h (50 mph).

If You Need Help. Call the number given in the car-hire documents. If you are a member of an AIT driving club or the AA, call the Automobile Association of Ireland: tel: 677 9481. The Royal Automobile Club (RAC) also has a breakdown number: tel: (toll-free) 800 535005.

E

ELECTRICITY

Ireland's standard electrical supply is 220 volts 50 cycles AC. Plugs are 3-pin flat or 2-pin round. If you need a travel adaptor, bring one with you.

EMBASSIES AND CONSULATES

Get in touch with the consulate of your home country if something disastrous happens – for example, if you lose your passport, get into trouble with the authorities or have an accident. The Consul can issue emergency passports, give advice on obtaining money from home, and provide a list of lawyers and doctors. It's best to phone in advance to check opening hours. The following embassies have consulates on the premises:

Australia:	Fitzwilton House, Wilton Terrace, Dublin 2; tel: 664 5300; <www.australianembassy.ie>
Canada:	65 St Stephen's Green, Dublin 2; tel: 417 4100; <www.canadaeuropa.gc.ca/ireland/>

South Africa:	Earlsfort Centre, Dublin 2; tel: 661 5553.
UK:	29 Merrion Road, Dublin 4; tel: 205 3700; <www.britishembassy.ie>
US:	42 Elgin Road, Dublin 4; tel: 668 8777; <www.usembassy.ie>

EMERGENCIES (See also HEALTH AND MEDICAL CARE and POLICE)

In the event of an emergency, dial 999 or 112 for Police, Ambulance, Fire and Coastguard. The call is free from all pay- and card phones.

G

GAY AND LESBIAN TRAVELLERS

Legislation ending the laws that criminalised male homosexuality was only passed in 1993. The repeal of these laws has brought about many changes in the gay scene. Though still small, the gay and lesbian community is now both visible and welcoming to visitors. The monthly newspaper, *Gay Community News* <www.gcn.ie> is widely available, and there are listings and features in *In Dublin*. Annual gay events are Mardi Gras (end of May), Pride (late June), and the Lesbian and Gay Film Festival (in the Irish Film Centre, end of July).

Help and information lines include Gay Switchboard Dublin; tel: 872 1055; Lesbian Line; tel: 872 9911. Outhouse (105 Capel Street, Dublin 2; tel: 873 4932; <www.outhouse.ie>) is a meeting place for the lesbian and gay community.

GETTING THERE (See also AIRPORT)

By Air. Ireland's national airline is Aer Lingus, which operates daily direct flights to Dublin from Boston/Logan, Chicago/O'Hare, Newark, Los Angeles and New York/JFK in the US; and from Birmingham, Bristol, Edinburgh, Glasgow, Leeds/Bradford, London/Heathrow/ Gatwick/City, Manchester and Newcastle in the UK; major air connections from the Continent include Amsterdam, Berlin, Brussels, Copenhagen, Frankfurt, Geneva, Madrid, Munich, Paris, Prague, Rome/da Vinci and Vienna.

Ireland's other national airline, Ryanair <www.ryanair.com> operates no-frills budget flights to Dublin from London/Gatwick/ Luton/Stansted, Aberdeen, Birmingham, Bournemouth, Bristol, Cardiff, Edinburgh, Glasgow Prestwick, Leeds, Liverpool, Manchester and Teeside.

From the US there are also direct flights to Dublin on Continental from JFK and Newark; and on Delta from Atlanta. Visitors flying from Australia, Canada, New Zealand or South Africa must make connections through London or another British hub with Aer Lingus, British Airways, British Midlands or Ryanair. Connections can also be made through another European hub: Air France, Lufthansa and Alitalia fly to Dublin.

There is a wide range of special promotional fares to Ireland (Ryanair offers many inexpensive fares to Britain), and discounts are available for senior citizens and students holding a valid International Student Identity Card. The cheapest fares on regular flights are APEX (advance purchase excursion) and super APEX, which must be booked and paid for three to four weeks in advance.

Packages that include a hotel room generally offer the best rates and conditions. A wide range of package tours or special-interest holidays are available, including fly-drive, sporting and activity holidays, and short breaks. A reliable travel agent can advise you on the best deals.

By Bus. Bus services linking Britain and Dublin are operated by Bus Eireann <www.buseireann.ie>, Ireland's national bus company (Travel Centre, Busáras, Store Street, Dublin 1; tel: 836 6111), in conjuction with Eurolines <www.eurolines.ie> via Dublin Ferryport and Dun Laoghaire upon Stena Line or Irish Ferries. Routes connect London and other major British towns to Dublin's central bus station, Busáras.

Most routes run daily, but some are seasonal so you should contact your travel agent for the latest information.

Countrywide bus services throughout Ireland are also provided by Bus Éireann. Departures are from Busáras (the central bus station), located in Store Street.

By Ferry. There are two main ferry companies. Irish Ferries runs ships from Dublin Port to Holyhead (tel: (1890) 313131 for information and reservations in Ireland; tel: (08705) 171717 in the UK <www.irish-ferries.com>); Stena Sealink operates boats from the Ferry Terminal in Dun Laoghaire to Holyhead. They offer both a regular service and a high-speed service that takes about half the normal time. For Stena Sealink reservations and information in Ireland; tel: 204 7777; in the UK; tel: (08705) 707070. Irish Ferries also sails from Rosslare to Le Havre and Cherbourg.

GUIDED TOURS

Bus Tours. City sightseeing tours by bus provide an excellent introduction to Dublin. Dublin Bus (59 Upper O'Connell Street, Dublin 1; tel: 873 4222; <www.dublinbus.ie>) operates a city tour that takes in the principal sights; in good weather, the tour is by open-top bus. The tour guides are entertaining, you can hop on or off at any of the stops, and your ticket is valid all day. Irish City Tours <www.irishcity tours.com> has a similar service, with tickets available on the bus. Dublin Bus also has an amusing, offbeat Ghost Bus Tour in the evening.

Bus Éireann runs day trips out of the city to sights such as Glendalough, Newgrange and the Boyne Valley, Russborough House and Powerscourt Gardens, as well as further afield. All tours depart from the Travel Centre at Busáras *(see page 113)*.

Gray Line Tours (Dublin Tourism Centre, Suffolk Street, Dublin 2; tel: 605 7705) offers a similar range of excursions. Tours depart from the Gray Line desk at the Dublin Tourism Centre and from a number of hotels.

Walking Tours. Dublin Tourism has signposted three self-guided walking tours, which you can enjoy at your own speed. The Cultural Heritage Trail covers Dublin north of the Liffey, while the Old City Heritage Trail heads east from Trinity College through Temple Bar to Dublin Castle. The Georgian Heritage Trail focuses on the city south of the river around St Stephen's Green, Fitzwilliam and Merrion Squares, and includes the National Gallery, National Museum and National Library. All three routes are best followed in conjunction with the detailed Heritage Trail booklets available at Suffolk Street. The Rock'n'Stroll Trail, for music fans, points out places associated with such artists as Bob Geldof, U2, Sinead O'Connor and the Chieftains, among others. Dublin Tourism also publishes The Dublin Touring Guide, with walks around the city and excursions on public transport.

The enjoyable Jameson Literary Pub Crawl, comprises an evening of readings, song and performance following in the footsteps of James Joyce, Samuel Beckett, Brendan Behan and others; tel: 878 0227 <www.historicalinsights.ie> or book at the Dublin Tourism Centre. The Musical Pub Crawl is led by a couple of professional musicians – they play and sing and talk about the history of Irish music. You can book at the Tourism Centre or tel: 478 0193 <www.musicalpub crawl.com>, and join the group at the Oliver St John Gogarty pub in Temple Bar.

No booking is required for the Literary/Georgian Walk, run by Dublin Footsteps; tel: 496 0641. Tours begin at the James Joyce Room in Bewley's on Grafton Street. Other tours can be booked by arrangement. Tours are available during the summer only.

The International Bar on Wicklow Street is the meeting place for the daily 1916 Rebellion Walking Tour taking in the most important sights of the Easter Rising. To book; tel: 676 2493; <www.1916 rising.com>. A Ghostly tour begins outside Dublin Castle every evening. The Zozimus Ghostly Experience visits the scenes of murders and myths. Book online <www.zozimus.com> or tel: 661 8646.

Wet and Dry Tours. Viking Splash Tours <www.vikingsplash tours.com> depart from Bull Alley Street just beside St Patrick's Cathedral in a vehicle that is not only an eye-catcher but is able to take you along the canals and rivers of Dublin as well as the streets.

There are many other tours available. You'll find more information at the Dublin Tourism Centre in Suffolk Street, and most outings can be booked there.

H

HEALTH AND MEDICAL CARE

Visitors who are not covered by their medical insurance should take out a short-term holiday policy before setting out: US citizens should note that Medicare does not cover them while they are abroad. Citizens of EU countries are covered by a reciprocal agreement and may use the Irish health services for medical treatment and hospital stays. British visitors should make sure they have an E111 form.

In the event of an accident, dial 999 or 112 for an ambulance. Your hotel or guesthouse proprietor will contact a doctor in an emergency, or you can call your consulate for advice. You can also contact the Irish Medical Organisation at 10 Fitzwilliam Place, Dublin 2; tel: 676 7273 for a recommendation. Beaumont Hospital, Beaumont Road, Dublin 9; tel: 809 2714, has a 24-hour emergency room. For non-emergency services, try the Grafton Street Centre on Grafton Street; tel: 671 2122.

If you need emergency dental treatment, call the Irish Dental Association, 10 Richview Office Park, Clonskeagh Road, Dublin 14; tel: 283 0499, which will be able to recommend a dentist.

Pharmacies (drugstores) are generally open during normal business hours. You can find the address of the nearest late-night pharmacy in the local press and under 'Chemists – Pharmaceutical' in the phone directory. There are branches of Boots Chemists on Grafton Street. Chemists on O'Connell Street tend to stay open quite late.

HOLIDAYS

Shops, banks, official departments and restaurants are closed on public holidays. If a holiday falls on a Sunday, the following Monday is normally taken instead. Although Good Friday is not officially a public holiday, it is observed as such in most of Ireland.

1 January	New Year's Day
17 March	St Patrick's Day
25 December	Christmas Day
26 December	St Stephen's Day
Movable Dates	
March/April	Good Friday/Easter Monday
First Monday in June	Whit or June Holiday
First Monday in August	Summer BankHoliday
Last Monday in October	All Souls

I

INTERNET CAFÉS

There seem to be Internet cafés around every corner. You shouldn't have to pay over €4 per hour. Planet Cyber on St Andrew Street is conveniently near the Dublin Tourist Office, but expensive. The Global Internet Cafe is equally overpriced, but is centrally located on O'Connell Street and provides left luggage facilities and phone cards.

L

LANGUAGE

Ireland is officially bilingual, as you'll see from the signs, and on official occasions either English or Irish may be used. English is spoken in Dublin and throughout most of Ireland; Irish is the main language in the areas designated as *Gaeltacht*. However, Irish is a required school subject, so most Irish people have knowledge of it. Signs around Dublin are usually self-explanatory. On buses, *An Lár* means 'City Centre.'

M

MAPS

For detailed maps of Dublin and the area around it, try the *Dublin Street Atlas and Guide*, available in bookstores, or buy a similar mini-atlas. If you need less detail, the tourism office gives out, free, *The Dublin Map*: useful as all attractions are plotted on it.

MEDIA

Radio and TV. The national broadcasting authority is RTE *(Radio Telefís Éireann)* which runs several TV channels, rte1 and Network 2, and three radio stations, RTE1, 2FM, and Lyric FM. TG4 is a television station with programmes in Irish. There is also an independent station, TV3. Television programmes from Britain via the BBC and ITV (independent television) can be received in the Dublin area, as well as all the BBC radio stations. Many hotels and some guesthouses are equipped to receive satellite television programmes via CNN, Sky TV and other operators.

Newspapers and Magazines. The *Irish Times* is the leading national daily, with interesting articles and a useful Notices section. The *Irish Independent* has more Ireland-focused coverage and publishes a special Sunday edition. The *Herald,* hawked at numerous street corners, is Dublin's local tabloid, with an extensive *Classifieds* section. Most newsagents stock the main UK national dailies, plus the Irish edition of London's *Sunday Times*, and many sell American and European newspapers. Foreign newspapers and periodicals can be purchased at Easons, located at 40–42 Lower O'Connell Street.

For what's going on, buy *In Dublin*, a good events listings magazine. The *Dublin Event Guide* is a free biweekly newspaper giving detailed coverage of what's on where. Also, Irish Tourism has several free publications that give useful restaurant reviews and up-to-date information on tourist attractions.

MONEY

Currency. Ireland's monetary unit is the euro (€), which is divided into 100 cent (¢).
Coins: 1¢, 2¢, 5¢, 10¢, 20¢, 50¢, €1 and €2.
Notes: €5, €10, €20, €50 and €100.

Changing money. For the best exchange rate, visitors should use banks, post offices and bureaux de change. The best rates are often obtained by using a credit card. Note that the Bank of Ireland ATMs charge for transactions with foreign banks.

Credit cards and travellers' cheques. Credit cards are accepted in most hotels, restaurants, petrol stations and large shops. Some guesthouses may not accept credit cards, so be sure to ask before booking. Travellers' cheques, supported by identification, can be exchanged at most banks or main travel service offices.

OPENING HOURS

Banks are usually open 10am–4pm Monday–Friday and 10am–5pm on Thursday; nearly all are open at lunchtime. Later closing times are gradually being introduced throughout Ireland.

Some shops follow Dublin's normal opening hours: Monday–Saturday 9/9.30am–5.30/6pm, with late-night shopping on Thursday until 8pm. A few suburban shopping centres stay open until 9pm on Thursday or Friday. In tourist areas hours are usually extended, and most places in Grafton Street remain open well into the evening and on Sunday. Many small groceries have late night opening and there are a few 24-hour shops in inner suburbs such as Rathmines/Ranelagh in the south and Phibsboro/Cabra in the north.

Most pubs are open all day from 10.30am until 12.30am, with a slightly later opening on Sunday, and earlier closing in winter.

P

POLICE

The emergency number for the Gardai is 999 or 112. Garda Headquarters is at 2 Hanover Street, Dublin 2; tel: 666 000.

POST OFFICES

Post office branches are open Monday–Friday 9am–5.30pm, and Saturday 9am–1pm. There is a post office at Dublin Airport, and a convenient branch is off Grafton Street on South Anne Street. Mailboxes are painted green and have the word 'Post' in yellow on the top. Dublin's main post office is the General Post Office (GPO) in O'Connell Street. It is open 8am–8pm Monday–Saturday and for stamps only on Sunday 10.30am–6pm. It handles mail, public telex, fax and telephone services. Many post offices exchange foreign currency and travellers' cheques.

PUBLIC TRANSPORT

Bus. The city's bus network is operated by Dublin Bus (Bus Átha Cliath), which is a subsidiary of the national transport company, CIE. The head office is at 59 O'Connell Street, Dublin 1 (tel: 873 4222 <www.dublinbus.ie>). Their green single- and double-deckers serve the city and the Greater Dublin area. Bus stops are frequent, and destinations and bus numbers are indicated at the front of the bus above the driver's window. Services include CitySwift (white and blue single-decker buses) and Imp (yellow and red minibuses) on some routes. Buses run from 6am–11.30pm. On popular routes, buses run every 10–20 minutes, but service on other routes could be much less frequent. There is a special hourly Nitelink service to the suburbs from 12.30–3.30am Thursday, Friday and Saturday (buses depart from College, D'Olier and Westmoreland streets every hour; buy your tickets from the van on College Street). A frequent bus service links Heuston Station and Busáras with Dublin airport. You need to have the right change ready unless you have a special pass (see below), which should be inserted into the validator as you enter the bus on the right hand side (combined bus/DART tickets should be shown to the driver/conductor). If you over pay, the driver will print you a credit slip. Collect these and they will refund you money at the headquarters on O'-Connell Street.

Fares. There are no flat fares on public transport, and the amount you pay depends on where you want to go. Fares range from €0.75–1.65. A range of discount passes are valid for bus or combined bus-and-rail. The one-day adult bus ticket allows unlimited travel for one day on all Dublin Bus services (except Nitelink). The one-day short-hop bus/rail ticket allows unlimited transport on Dublin Bus and DART for one person (except on Nitelink) for one day, while the family one-day ticket extends the same concessions to two adults and up to four children under 16. The Dublin Explorer Ticket is valid for four consecutive days on bus and DART after 9.45am Monday–Friday, with no weekend restrictions. Seven-day passes are also available for unlimited travel on the bus, commencing on a Sunday (photo ID required). There are also a variety of student and children's passes. Passes can be obtained from the Dublin Bus booking office at 59 O'Connell Street or from any bus ticket agent.

Rail/DART. Dublin Area Rapid Transit (DART) provides a swift and efficient electrified rail link through the city, from the seaside towns of Howth in the north and Greystones in the south. The line runs along the Dublin Bay coast and serves a total of 28 stations. Trains run approximately every 15 minutes (every 5 minutes during rush hours) 7am–midnight Monday–Saturday, and 9.30am–11pm Sunday. Avoid travelling at peak times when trains are packed with commuters.

Taxi. The place to get a taxi is at one of the many clearly marked taxi ranks located outside major hotels, bus and railway stations, and on busy thoroughfares. Taxis don't normally cruise for business. There are 24-hour taxi ranks at Aston Quay, College Green, Eden Quay, O'Connell Street and St Stephen's Green (East and North). At busy times there can be a long wait. You can also order a taxi by calling a specific company; look in the Golden Pages of the telephone directory under 'Taxicabs.' You will probably have to pay a pick-up charge if you order a taxi by phone.

Taxis are identified by a sign giving the name of the firm and their number on the car roof. Rates are fixed by law and displayed in all taxis. They are valid for a 16-km (10-mile) radius outside the city; beyond that, fares should be negotiated in advance with the driver.

R

RELIGION

Ireland is predominantly a Roman Catholic country, but other religions are represented in Dublin. For a list of services, look in the Saturday edition of the *Irish Times*.

Roman Catholic. Pro-Cathedral, Marlborough Street; tel: 874 5441.
Church of Ireland. Christ Church Cathedral, Edward Square; tel: 677 8099. St Patrick's Cathedral, Patrick Street; tel: 453 9472
Methodist. Dublin Central Mission, Abbey Street; tel: 874 0691
Muslim. Mosque and Islamic Centre, 163 South Circular Road, Dublin 8; tel: 454 3242
Unitarian. Unitarian Church, 112 St Stephen's Green West, Dublin 2; tel: 478 0638

T

TELEPHONES

The telephone dialling code for the Dublin area when calling from outside the city is 01; the code for Ireland is 353. In this book, numbers within Dublin are listed minus the code.The Irish telephone operator is called Eircom. Direct-dial local and international calls can be made from all hotels and most guesthouses or from any public phone. Bear in mind that any calls made from a hotel will have a hefty surcharge.

To make a call within Dublin, dial only the seven-digit number. To call Dublin from another place in Ireland, dial the 01 area code plus the seven-digit number. To reach Northern Ireland, dial 048, the area code, and the number. The access number for international calls is 00, followed by the country code: 61 for Australia, 64 for New Zealand, 27 for South Africa, 44 for the UK, and 1 for the US. Pay-phone international calls are cheaper after 6pm Monday–Friday and at any time over the weekend.

Though there are still some coin phones, telephone calling cards are widely used; you can buy them in units of 10, 20, 50 or 100 from post offices, newsstands or shops displaying a phone card notice. To use a phone card, listen for the dial tone, insert the card in the direction of the arrow, and dial the number. A display will show you how many units are left on the card, and when your card runs out, you will hear a beeping sound. To make a call on a coin phone, dial the number first, and wait until you are connected before you put in the coins. Note that mobile (cell) phones from the US will not work in Ireland.

To call directory enquiries for Ireland, dial 11811; for British and other international calls, dial 11818. This service isn't free, but you are entitled to make up to three inquiries per call. For an international operator, dial 114; for a local or British operator, dial 10. Dial 196 to send a telegram.

If you need to make a lot of calls, Eircom has retail outlets on O'Connell Street and on King Street near Grafton where you can make calls from comfortable indoor facilities.

TICKETS

The Dublin Tourism Centre in Suffolk Street will book tickets to theatre, concerts and other events. Also contact Ticketmaster; tel: 456 9569; <www.ticketmaster.ie>. The following accept credit card bookings: Andrews Lane Theatre; tel: 679 5720; the Gaiety; tel: 677 1717; the Gate; tel: 874 4045; and the Olympia; tel: 677 7744.

TIME ZONES

Ireland follows Greenwich Mean Time (GMT: 1 hour earlier than Central European Time) from November to March and summer time (the same as Britain) from April to October. Ireland's latitude means that summer days are long (it's light until around 11pm), and that daylight hours in mid-winter are quite short (it's dark by 3.30pm).

New York	**Dublin**	Paris	Jo'burg	Sydney
7am	noon	1pm	2pm	10pm

TIPPING

Hotel bills usually include a service charge. If a service charge is included in a restaurant bill, tipping is not obligatory unless service has been exceptional. If you're not sure whether a service charge has been added, ask; if it isn't included, give 10 percent. Give your hairdresser/barber about 10 percent; porters €1–2 per bag; taxi drivers 10 percent.

TOILETS

Dublin is not well provided with public conveniences. Around Grafton Street, the shopping centres and Marks & Spencer have toilets on their top floors; there are toilets downstairs in the Trinity College Arts Building inside the Nassau Street gate. Use the facilities in museums, department stores or pubs. Toilets may be labelled with symbols, or with the words *Fir* for men and *Mna* for women.

TOURIST INFORMATION

Before you leave home, you can get information from the Irish National Tourist Board – **Bord Fáilte** (literally 'Board of Welcomes'),

which maintains offices throughout the world. The main
office is at Baggot Street Bridge, Dublin 2; information tel: 602 4000;
<www.ireland.travel.ie>.

Australia: 36 Carrington Street, Sydney NSW 2000;
tel: (02) 9299 6177

Canada: 2 Bloor Street West, Suite 1501, Toronto, Ontario
M4W 3E2; tel: (0800) 223 6470

New Zealand: 18 Shortland Street, Private Bag 92136, Auckland 1;
tel: (09) 379 8720

UK: 1 Regent Street, London SW1Y; tel: (0800) 039 7000

US: 345 Park Avenue, New York, NY 10154; tel: (800) 223 6470

When you arrive in Dublin, your first stop should be the **Dublin
Tourism Centre**, in Suffolk Street, Dublin 2 (information tel: 605
7700; <www.visitdublin.com>), located in the renovated St Andrews
church. They offer numerous services – a bureau de change, a car hire
agency, a desk for transport information, a café and a gift/bookshop.
They can book tours, theatre and concert tickets, and accommodation
(for a small charge), and have a wealth of brochures and other information. The centre is open all year Monday–
Saturday 9am–5.30pm, closed Sunday; hours are sometimes extended
in July and August. Other locations are at the following addresses:
Arrivals Building, Dublin International Airport (open: daily
8am–10pm); Exclusively Irish, O'Connell Street, Dublin 2; Dun
Laoghaire Ferry Terminal (open: daily 10am–9pm).

TRAVELLERS WITH DISABILITIES

While a number of hotels and guesthouses have adapted their facilities to cater for visitors with special needs, most historic buildings
and museums do not provide wheelchair access.

The **National Rehabilitation Board** (25 Clyde Road, Dublin 4;
tel: 668 4181) publishes an accommodation guide and fact sheets
which indicate where wheelchair access and other facilities are available. Both are free and can be obtained from the Irish Tourist Board.

W

WEBSITES

Information on the web can help you get ready for your trip to Dublin. There are many sites where you can find deals on airfares, hotels and car hire: <www.expedia.com> also has sites in Australia, Canada, and the UK; if you're travelling from the US try <www.bestfares.com> and <www.travelocity.com>. You can make hotel guesthouse or B&B reservations at <www.goireland.com>. The Irish Hotels Federation has a site at <www.beourguest.ie>.

For sightseeing and other general information: <www.travel.ireland.ie> is the excellent site of the Irish Tourist Board; Dublin Tourism's site is <www.visitdublin.ie>; Dúchas, the Heritage Services, also has a site; <www.heritageireland.ie>. You can look at *In Dublin* at <www.indublin.ie> to see what's going on, or try <www.indigo.ie>; The *Irish Times* is at <www.ireland.com>.

WEIGHTS AND MEASURES

Ireland transferred to the metric system some time ago, although there are still hangovers from the past: milk comes in pints as well as litres and cars still tend to have speedometers in miles rather than kilometres.

Y

YOUTH HOSTELS

Members of the Independent Holiday Hostels of Ireland operate 19 hostels in and around Dublin. Many are open all year, and provide storage lockers, information desks, laundry facilities and bike hire as well as accommodation. The headquarters are located at 57 Lower Gardiner Street; tel: 836 4700; fax: 836 4710; <www.hostels ireland.com>.

Recommended Hotels

The standard of service in hotels and guesthouses can vary considerably. There is sometimes little difference between hotels and guesthouses, but the latter are usually cheaper, and city centre hotels, especially in Temple Bar, are usually more noisy.

Listed below is a selection of hotels in four price categories, grouped in the following areas: Dublin city centre, north suburbs, south suburbs and south coast. Although the tourist information offices at Dublin Airport and Suffolk Street have hotel booking facilities, you are advised to book your accommodation well in advance, either through a travel agent or directly with the hotel.

Many hotels add a service charge to the quoted price, and some establishments charge more during special events. Be sure to ask what is included in the quoted rates: Ask about VAT (government tax), service and breakfast (after a full Irish breakfast you probably won't need lunch). Also ask about special weekend rates and other special offers.

As a basic guide to room prices, we have used the following symbols for a double room with bath or shower (en suite), usually including breakfast, service charge and tax:

€€€€	over 250 euros
€€€	200–250 euros
€€	100–200 euros
€	below 100 euros

CITY CENTRE

Blooms Hotel €€ *6 Anglesea Street, Temple Bar, Dublin 2; tel: 671 5622; fax: 671 5997; <www.blooms.ie>*. A convenient modern hotel in the Temple Bar area, Blooms is a perfect choice for party-goers, but not for those planning a quiet night. Downstairs is Club M, one of Dublin's hottest nightclubs.

Buswells Hotel € *23–27 Molesworth Street, Dublin 2; tel: 614 6500; fax: 676 2090;* *<www.quinnhotels.com>*. Centrally located (opposite the National Museums complex) in a former Georgian townhouse, Buswells has an old-world atmosphere and period furnishings. Conference facilities. 69 rooms.

Castle Hotel € *2–4 Gardiner Row, Dublin 1; tel: 874 6949; fax: 872 7674; email:* *<hotels@indigo.ie>*. The Castle Hotel consists of three adjacent and tastefully restored Georgian buildings, close to Parnell Square. Authentically restored décor combined with modern comfort. Small conference facilities and parking. 38 rooms.

Central Hotel € *1–5 Exchequer Street, Dublin 2; tel: 679 7302; fax: 679 7303;* *<www.centralhotel:ie>*. A comfortable hotel right beside Temple Bar, decorated and furnished in Victorian style. Dining room, bars, conference facilities. 70 rooms.

Clarence Hotel €€€€ *6–8 Wellington Quay, Dublin 2; tel: 407 0800; fax: 407 0820;* *<www.theclarence.ie>*. Located in a handsome hotel built in 1852. Recently renovated, each room is uniquely designed in a contemporary manner. Adjacent to Temple Bar and overlooking the River Liffey, its nightclub is one of Dublin's finest. Parking. 50 rooms.

Conrad International Dublin €€€€ *Earlsfort Terrace, Dublin 2; tel: 602 8900; fax: 676 5424;* *<www.conraddublin.com>*. Situated just off St Stephen's Green, this glass construction opposite the National Concert Hall houses one of Ireland's few five-star hotels. The Conrad's two restaurants, traditional pub and elegant tea room could make it difficult to leave. Full business and conference facilities. Car park. 191 rooms.

Davenport Hotel €€€€ *Merrion Square, Dublin 2; tel: 607 3500; fax: 661 5663;* *<www.davenport.ie>*. The neoclassical style of the impressive facade of this elegant 1860s building is carried over into its vast atrium lobby. Fine-dining restaurant, bar, conference facilities, car park. 115 rooms.

Fitzsimmons Hotel €€ *21–22 Wellington Quay, Dublin 2; tel: 677 9315; fax: 677 9387; <www.fitzsimonshotel.com>.* If you're coming to Dublin to experience a weekend you'll soon forget (ie a weekends with the lads/lasses) this is the place for you. You won't get much sleep, but there's plenty of time for that on the plane. A huge night club and one of Temple Bar's best pubs make this hotel an all night affair. 26 rooms.

Fitzwilliam Hotel €€€€ *St Stephen's Green, Dublin 2; tel: 478 7000; fax: 478 7878; www.fitzwilliam.com>.* This upmarket modern hotel, located on the Green, has a contemporary and understated elegance. There are views of Dublin from the lovely roof garden. Its restaurant, Conrad Gallagher's Peacock Alley, is one of Dublin's finest. Rooms have all amenities and comforts. Conference facilities, parking. 130 rooms.

Grafton Capital €€ *Stephens Street Lower, Dublin 2; tel: 648 1100; fax: 648 1122; <www.capital-hotels.com>.* This is the showpiece in Capital's Dublin hotels. Very reasonably priced considering the excellent service and room size, and you can't get any nearer the nightlife than this. Like many Capital hotels, a popular nightclub snuggles into the hotel. Across the road a string of Dublin's best cafés wait to help you recover the morning after. 75 rooms.

Gresham Hotel €€ *23 Upper O'Connell Street, Dublin 1; tel: 874 6881; fax: 878 7175; <www.gresham-hotels.com>.* One of Dublin's legendary hotels, the Gresham is based in the heart of the city, near the General Post Office. The fine, early 19th-century building, with its marble floors and large rooms offers luxurious accommodation. Restaurant and two bars, conference facilities, parking. 288 rooms.

Longfields Hotel €€ *9–10 Lower Fitzwilliam Street, Dublin 2; tel: 676 1367; fax: 676 1542; <www.longfields.ie>.* Wonderfully located in a splendid Georgian building near Merrion and Fitzwilliam squares, this stylish hotel offers period furnishings, an excellent restaurant and a bar. 26 rooms.

Merrion Hotel €€€€ *Upper Merrion Street, Dublin 2; tel: 603 0600; fax: 603 0700; <www.merrionhotel.com>.* This elegant hotel was created from four Georgian town houses. Its gracious setting overlooking an 18th-century garden, its discreet service, and its beautifully appointed rooms and suites offer an outstanding experience. One of Dublin's notable restaurants, Patrick Guilbaud *(see page 137)* is located here, as well as bars, spa and health club. Conference facilities, parking. 145 rooms.

Mont Clare Hotel €€ *Merrion Square, Dublin 2; tel: 607 3800; fax: 661 5663; <www.ocallaghanhotels.ie>.* An attractive hotel with a traditional club-like feel, in a Georgian building on lovely Merrion Square. Convenient for the National Art Gallery, Trinity College and other attractions. Restaurant and bar. Business facilities, car park. 74 rooms.

The Morgan €€€ *10 Fleet Street, Temple Bar, Dublin 2; tel: 679 3939; fax: 679 3946; <www.themorgan.com>.* Simply the most stylish hotel in Temple Bar. You should stay here if you've come to live it up or seduce. You shouldn't stay here if your idea of an Irish night out is a cup of Barry's tea and some shortbread. 61 rooms

Morrison Hotel €€€ *Lower Ormond Quay, Dublin 1; tel: 887 2400; fax: 878 3185; <www.morrisonhotel.ie>.* A modern building overlooking the River Liffey it's one of Dublin's most sophisticated hotels. It comes with its own bar, café, restaurant and, like many in Temple Bar, a night club. 91 rooms.

Number 31 €€ *31 Leeson Close, Dublin 2; tel: 676 5011; fax: 676 2929; <www.number31.ie>.* For an upscale B&B with little advertising and no trace of a sign outside, you may wonder why it's so difficult to find a room. The answer is simple: spacious rooms, listed architecture (Georgian or modern, take your pick), and a breakfast that will make you want to spend every night here. 18 rooms.

Royal Dublin Hotel €€ *O'Connell Street, Dublin 1; tel: 873 3666; fax: 873 3120; <www.royaldublin.com>.* Near Parnell

Square, this hotel is close to the Gate Theatre, Hugh Lane Gallery and Writers' Museum. The public rooms are Georgian; the ensuite bedrooms contemporary. Restaurant and bars, car park. 117 rooms.

Russell Court Hotel €€ *Harcourt Street, Dublin 2; tel: 478 4066; fax: 478 1576.* Two Georgian houses make up this hotel with its Victorian-style décor. A new wing has added six rooms. Restaurant, new nightclub and bars. 52 rooms.

Shelbourne Hotel €€€€ *27 St Stephen's Green, Dublin 2; tel: 663 4500; fax: 661 6006; <www.shelbourne.ie>.* Dublin's most famous hotel is known for its distinction and elegant charm. Some rooms overlook the Green, and all are furnished for style and comfort with every amenity. A very good restaurant and bar; the lobby is a favourite place to meet for afternoon tea. Meeting rooms, new leisure centre, car park. 103 rooms.

Staunton's on the Green € *83 St Stephen's Green South, Dublin 2; tel: 478 2300; fax: 478 2263; email: <hotels@indigo.ie>.* This exclusive Georgian guesthouse, with its splendid high ceilings and windows, overlooks St Stephen's Green in front and the Iveagh Gardens to the rear. The charming, spacious rooms are all en suite with telephone. 30 rooms.

Stephen's Green Hotel €€€€ *St Stephen's Green, Dublin 2; tel: 607 3600; fax: 661 5663; <www.ocallaghanhotels.ie>.* This boutique hotel, on the west side of the Green, looks strikingly modern and offers every amenity including a four-storey glass atrium overlooking the Green. Restaurant, bar, meeting rooms. 75 rooms.

Temple Bar Hotel € *Fleet Street, Temple Bar, Dublin 2; tel: 677 3333; fax: 677 3088; <www.towerhotelgroup.ie>.* This pleasant hotel is in Temple Bar, near clubs and pubs, and a stone's throw away from Grafton Street. Restaurant and bar; meeting rooms; Buskers Theme Bar next door. 129 rooms.

Wynn's Hotel €€ *35–39 Lower Abbey Street, Dublin 1; tel: 874 5131; fax: 874 1556; <www.wynnshotel.ie>.* This city centre hotel is just around the corner from the Abbey Theatre. Recently refurbished. Restaurant, bar, conference facilities, parking. 70 rooms.

Trinity Lodge €€ *12 South Frederick Street, Dublin 2; tel: 679 5044; fax: 679 5223; <www.trinitylodge.com>.* Tucked along one of the best hidden streets in Dublin you can't get anymore central than this and it's difficult to find a quieter location. Inside the rooms are full of wooden furniture and big, comfy beds. Outside you are next door to one of Dublin's best café society areas. 10 rooms.

Trinity Capital €€ *Pearse Street, Dublin 2; tel: 648 1000; fax: 648 1010; <www.capital-hotels.com>.* One of several Capital Hotels in the city. Their slogan is 'individual hotels for individual people'. This is perfect for the no frills individual who can't afford a night in its nearby sister the Grafton Capital. 81 rooms.

NORTH OF THE CENTRE

Chief O'Neill's Hotel €€€ *Smithfield Village, Dublin 7; tel: 817 3838; fax: 817 3839; <www.chiefoneills.com>.* Located in the same complex as the Jameson Distillery, and sporting a lookout tower and outdoor lighting that attempts sculpture, one suspects this area may be on to something. It's hard to remember this when waiting for the bus to all the 'good bits' of Dublin, but every incredibly stylish room comes with a free CD. Chief O'Neill was a voracious collector of Irish music. 73 rooms.

Egan's Guesthouse € *7–9 Iona Park, Glasnevin, Dublin 9; tel: 830 3611; fax: 830 3312; <www.eganshouse.com>.* This is a very pleasant Victorian residence near the splendid Botanic Gardens, Croke Park and the airport. Car park. 23 rooms.

Regency Airport Hotel € *Swords Road, Whitehall, Dublin 9; tel: 837 3544; fax: 836 7121; <www.regencyhotels.com>.* A great place to stay if you're coming in too late for the fun or too early for the sun. Located between the city and the airport, the rooms are modern and its theme restaurant will feed you well. 212 rooms.

SOUTH OF THE CENTRE

Bewley's Hotel Ballsbridge € *Merrion Road, Ballsbridge, Dublin 4; tel: 668 1111; fax: 668 1999; <www.BewleysHotels.com>.* A new, spacious, and strikingly modern hotel behind a restored 1793 facade. It offers very reasonably priced deluxe rooms and suites. Restaurant, bar, car park. 220 rooms.

Burlington Hotel €€ *Upper Leeson Street, Dublin 4; tel: 660 5222; fax: 660 8496; <www.jurysdoyle-hotel.com>.* A huge and popular hotel, the Burlington has Dublin's largest conference facilities. Restaurants, nightclubs, shops, car park. 504 rooms.

Glenveagh Townhouse € *31 Northumberland Road, Ballsbridge, Dublin 4; tel: 668 4612; fax: 668 4559.* A pleasant Victorian house offering ensuite rooms in a quiet location. Parking. 10 rooms.

Hibernian Hotel €€ *Eastmoreland Place, Ballsbridge, Dublin 4; tel: 668 7666; fax: 660 2655; <www.hibernianhotel.com>.* A luxury hotel in an early 20th-century townhouse with an old-world atmosphere. Nearby sports and other facilities are complimentary to guests. Conference facilities, car park. 40 rooms.

Lansdowne Hotel € *27–29 Pembroke Road, Ballsbridge, Dublin 4; tel: 668 2522; fax: 668 5585; <www.lansdownehotel.com>.* Set back from a tree-lined road in Ballsbridge. Celtic Restaurant, traditional bar, car park. 40 rooms.

Mount Herbert Hotel € *Herbert Road, Landsdowne Road, Dublin 4; tel: 668 4321; fax: 660 7077; <www.mountherberthotel.ie>.* A family-run hotel in a large, extended Victorian building with a children's play area, near Lansdowne Road DART. Functional but comfortable ensuite rooms. Restaurant, bar, conference facilities, parking. 185 rooms.

Rathmines Capital € *Lower Rathmines Road, Dublin 6; tel: 496 6966; fax: 491 0603; <www.capital-hotels.com>.* If you find yourself in Rathmines, the Capital is by far your best option. The club downstairs is trendy, the restaurant tasty and the rooms affordable. Easy access to the city if you don't mind the bus ride or prefer the student atmosphere over the city lights. 54 rooms.

Raglan Lodge € *10 Raglan Road, Ballsbridge, Dublin 4; tel: 660 6697; fax: 660 6781.* In a Victorian house dating from 1861, this hotel offers a quiet stay in a peaceful location 10 minutes by bus from Dublin's centre. Award-winning breakfast. Parking. 7 rooms.

Sachs Hotel € *19–29 Morehampton Road, Donnybrook, Dublin 4; tel: 668 0995; fax: 668 6147.* A pleasant, quiet hotel with spacious rooms. Leisure centre and nightclub, complimentary to guests; conference facilities and parking. 20 rooms.

Stephens Hall €€€ *Earlsfort Centre, Lower Leeson Street, Dublin 2; tel: 638 1111; fax: 638 1122; <www.choicehotelsireland.ie>.* This all-suite hotel is set in a row of Georgian terraced houses near the canal. It is particularly suitable for an extended stay: the suites comprise a small kitchen, dining area, sitting room, bathroom, and one or two bedrooms. There is a restaurant, and car parking is also available. 37 suites.

SOUTH COAST

Fitzpatrick Castle Hotel €€ *Killiney Hill Road, Killiney, Co. Dublin; tel: 230 5400; fax: 230 5466; <www.fitzpatrickhotels.com>.* This period residence sits in 3.5 hectares (9 acres) of landscaped gardens and wooded grounds, overlooking Dublin Bay. A courtesy bus (30 minutes) connects it with the city centre. Restaurant, bar, leisure centre, swimming pool, tennis courts and other sports facilities; golf available. Conference facilities and car park. 113 rooms.

Gresham Royal Marine Hotel €€–€€€ *Marine Road, Dun Laoghaire, Co. Dublin; tel: 280 1911; fax: 280 1089; <www.ryan hotels.com/htm/marine_i.htm>.* Close to the ferry port, with 1.5-hectare (4-acre) gardens, this is a fully restored and renovated Victorian building with a new wing. A 20-minute ride on the DART from the city centre. Meeting rooms, golf, car park. 104 rooms.

Recommended Restaurants

Dublin has a superb range of both traditional Irish and cosmopolitan restaurants. Most offer both fixed price and à la carte menus. A fixed-price three- or four-course meal is often the best value. Meal prices include 12.5 percent government tax (VAT), and a 15 percent service charge is often added to the final bill. Many restaurants offer early or pre-theatre dinners at reduced prices. Look for specials in local publications. Don't forget that most pubs offer good food, and some have dining rooms. Many museums and other attractions have excellent, moderately priced cafés.

As a basic guide, the following symbols give an idea of the price for an average meal for one, including a service charge of 10–15 percent but excluding wine or other drinks:

€€€€	above 30 euros
€€€	25–30 euros
€€	15–25 euros
€	below 15 euros

CITY CENTRE SOUTH

Bewley's Oriental Café € *Grafton Street, Dublin 2; tel: 677 6761.* Open daily from breakfast time until midnight. Come to this legendary Dublin spot at least once for the atmosphere: particularly the Grafton Street branch, with its old stained glass and wooden gargoyles. There is occasional entertainment in the evening, and the brunch is famous. The other branches can be found in Westmoreland Street, South Great George's Street and Mary Street.

The Bistro €€ *4–5 Castle Market, Dublin 2; tel: 671 5430.* Open Mon–Sat noon–10.30pm, Sun 1–8.30pm. An informal, good-value Italian restaurant which serves a wide range of excellent dishes, including generous pizzas. The atmosphere is friendly and children are welcome.

Cafe en Seine €€–€€€ *40 Dawson Street, Dublin 2; tel: 677 4369.* Open Sun–Wed 5pm–12.30am, Thur–Sat 3pm–12.30am. Stylish hangout for over a decade. Salads, steaks, pasta and simple dishes. Live jazz brunch on Sunday.

The Cedar Tree €€–€€€ *11a St Andrew Street, Dublin 2; tel: 677 2121.* Open Sun–Thur 5.30–10.45pm, Fri and Sat 5.30pm–12.30am. The Lebanese food here is authentic and reasonably priced, with good vegetarian options.

Chili Club €€ *1 Anne's Lane, off South Anne Street, Dublin 2; tel: 677 3721.* Open weekdays for lunch, daily for dinner. One of the oldest Thai restaurants in Dublin, with good, authentic food, served in a rather small, friendly setting. Some vegetarian options on an extensive menu.

The Commons €€€€ *Newman House, 85–86 St Stephen's Green South, Dublin 2; tel: 478 0530;* <www.thecommonsrestaurant.ie>. Open weekdays 12.30–2.15pm and 7–10.15pm, dinner only on Sat, closed Sun. In the basement of Newman House, with fine Georgian architectural detail and a really lovely terrace garden, Chef Aidan Byrne features a constantly changing menu of innovative dishes along with excellent service. One of the best and most popular formal restaurants in central Dublin. Tasting menu offered for a party.

Cornucopia € *19 Wicklow Street, Dublin 2; tel: 677 7583.* Open Mon–Fri 8.30am–8pm (until 9pm on Thur). The food is now better than ever at this favourite vegetarian restaurant. A small, informal place, mostly self-service, with table service weekend nights only. Visa is the only credit card accepted.

Fitzers Café €€ *Branches at 51 Dawson Street, 40 Temple Bar and in the National Gallery (Merrion Square West), Dublin 2.* Open daily noon–10.45pm except for the National Gallery branch, which keeps museum hours (and sometimes runs out of hot food at lunchtime). All branches are stylishly cool cafés serving a range of international dishes and a selection of cakes and tarts; vegetarian options.

Good World Restaurant €€ *18 South Great George's Street, Dublin 2; tel: 677 5373.* Open daily 12.30pm–3am. This is a popular place, with the best dim sum in the city. The cooking is good, and less geared to Western tastes than most.

Jewel in the Crown €€ *5 South William Street, Dublin 2; tel: 677 0681.* Mon–Sat 12.30–2.30pm and 4pm–midnight. A classic Indian restaurant centrally located. It has delicious food and attentive service – great value.

Juice €€ *73 South Great George's Street, Dublin 2; tel: 475 7856* Daily 12–11pm. Tasty vegetarian dishes. Organically produced wines, juice bar.

La Cave €€ *South Anne Street, Dublin 2; tel: 679 4409.* Open Mon–Sat noon–11pm, Sun 6–11pm. Dublin's oldest authentic French wine bar, with bistro-style dishes reasonably priced. It's decorated with nostalgic posters and prints, and – as you would expect – has an excellent wine list.

La Mère Zou €€€€ *22 St Stephen's Green, Dublin 2; tel/fax: 661 6669.* Open 6–10.30pm, until 11pm Fri–Sat and 10pm Sun. A beguiling, bright restaurant with a French country air, downstairs on the north side of the Green. Very good French food, delicious desserts and friendly service.

Pasta Fresca €–€€ *3–4 Chatham Street, Dublin 2; tel: 679 2402.* Open daily 11.30am–11.30pm. A popular and relaxed restaurant, serving, as the name suggests, virtually every possible combination of pasta and sauce. Ask about specials at lunchtime. Vegetarian options. Service can be slow.

Patrick Guilbaud €€€€ *46 St James's Place (off Lower Baggot Street), Dublin 2; tel: 676 4192.* Open for lunch and dinner, closed Sun–Mon. With two Michelin stars, this is Dublin's finest French restaurant, with commensurate prices. In the Merrion Hotel, the formal dining room serves a superb cuisine. The fixed-price lunch is the least expensive option. Reservations advised.

QV2 €€€€ *14–15 St Andrew's Street, Dublin 2; tel: 677 3363;* *<www.qv2restaurant.com>*. Open Mon–Sat noon–3pm and 6–11pm, closed Sun. A stylish and modern restaurant, popular with those 'in the know'. Contemporary cuisine. Facilities for private parties.

Rajdoot €€€ *26–28 Clarendon Street, Westbury Centre, Dublin 2; tel: 679 4280.* Open Mon–Fri 12.15–2.15pm, Sat 12.30–3pm, Sun 1.30–5.30pm and Mon–Sat 6.30–llpm, Sun 6.30–10pm. An award-winning Indian restaurant with a vast menu, much of which is suitable for vegetarians. Served in appropriately opulent surroundings and licensed.

Roly's Bistro €€€ *7 Ballsbridge Terrace, Dublin 4; tel: 668 2611.* Open noon–2.45pm and 5.30–9.45pm. Attractive bistro restaurant on two floors, with imaginative and well-presented menus, usually focused around original fish and meat dishes. Good service and a lively atmosphere.

Steps of Rome €€ *Chatham Street, Dublin 2; tel: 670 5630.* Open daily noon–11pm. This tiny restaurant has real, authentic pizza; the very best in Dublin. The service is friendly and relaxed, and you can take away. Get there early – there are only a few tables. No credit cards.

Thai Orchid €€ *7 Westmoreland Street, Dublin 2; tel: 671 9969; fax: 671 9968.* Open Mon–Fri for lunch 12.30–2.30pm, daily for dinner 5–11.30pm. Right across from Trinity College, this pleasant restaurant serves delicate and tasty authentic Thai cuisine.

The Trocadero €€–€€€ *3 St Andrew's Street, Dublin 2; tel: 677 5545.* Open daily 5pm–midnight. The Trocadero has long been known for its popularity with media types (including those in front of the camera). The reasonably priced food is competent but punters really come here for the atmosphere and people watching.

Yamamori Noodles €€–€€€ *71 South Great George's Street, Dublin 2; tel: 475 5001.* Open daily from 12.30pm closing at 11pm Su–Wed; 11.30pm Thur–Sat. Japanese restaurant and probably the best place for noodles in Dublin. The clientele is predominantly cool.

OLD TOWN/LIBERTIES

Les Frères Jacques €€€€ *74 Dame Street, Dublin 2; tel: 679 4555;<www.lesfreres jacques.com>*. Open daily 12.30–2.30pm and 7–10.30pm. Next to the Olympia Theatre, this small restaurant offers authentic French cuisine in a relaxed and pleasant setting.

Old Dublin Restaurant €€–€€€ *90–91 Francis Street, Dublin 8; tel: 454 2028*. Open daily noon–2.30pm and 6–11pm. Specializes in Russian and Scandinavian recipes such as *borscht, novgorod* (beef chateaubriand with fried barley and caviar), and *pelmini* (small beef or veal dumplings in consommé), using only fresh Irish produce. This unusual but long-established restaurant will set you up for antique hunting in Francis Street. Reservations suggested.

TEMPLE BAR

Bruno's €€ *30 East Essex Street, Dublin 2; tel: 670 6767*. Open Mon–Fri 12.30–2.30, Mon–Sat 6–10.30pm. Excellent, eclectic cooking and a lively crowd make this good-value restaurant an interesting place for lunch or dinner.

Elephant and Castle €–€€ *18 Temple Bar, Dublin 2; tel: 679 3121*. Open Mon–Fri 8am–11pm, Sat 10.30–11.30pm, Sun noon–11pm. Good food and reasonable prices have assured the continuing popularity of this informal place. Come here for quality burgers and salads as well as the famous spicy chicken wings, or for large helpings of sinful ice cream desserts. Vegetarian options are also available.

Gallagher's Boxty House €–€€ *20–21 Temple Bar, Dublin 2; tel: 677 2762*. Open daily noon–11pm. Boxty is an old Irish dish: potato pancakes stuffed with a variety of fillings (including vegetarian), served at long tables to traditional Irish background music; a must stop for every tourist.

The Shack Restaurant €€ *24 East Essex Street, Temple Bar, Dublin 2; tel: 679 0043.* Open daily 11am–11pm. This comfortable, attractive restaurant has good continental food, vegetarian selections, and excellent traditional Irish dishes.

CITY CENTRE NORTH

Chapter One Restaurant €€€€ *18–19 Parnell Square, Dublin 1; tel: 873 2266.* Open Tues–Fri 12.30–2.30pm, Tues–Sat 6–11pm. In the basement of the Dublin Writers Museum, this is one of the city's best, with excellent modern Irish dishes accompanied by fine wines. It's convenient to the Gate Theatre, and pre-theatre menus are available. Reservations advised.

101 Talbot €€€ *101–102 Talbot Street (Upstairs), Dublin 1; tel: 874 5011.* Open Tues–Sat 5–11pm. Don't be put off by the dingy neighbourhood – this popular restaurant serves excellent international food in generous portions. The staff are friendly, prices reasonable and there is a good wine list.

The Winding Stair € *40 Lower Ormond Quay, Dublin 1; tel: 873 3292.* Open Mon–Sat 10am–6pm, Sun 1–6pm. A café and book-shop in an 18th-century building with views over the River Liffey. It's popular, picturesque and full of books, but can become very crowded. The emphasis is on salads, soups and sandwiches. And it's not called the Winding Stair for nothing. No credit cards.

SOUTH SUBURBS

Ernie's €€€ *Mulberry Gardens, Donnybrook, Dublin 4; tel: 269 3300.* Open Tues–Sat 12.30–2pm and 7.30–10pm. An interesting restaurant, built around a mulberry tree, with the main dining room lined with contemporary Irish paintings. The cooking and presenta-tion is classical; food is cooked on a charcoal grill, and seafood and game are available in season.

La Finezza €€€ *Over Kiely's, 22–24 Donnybrook Road, Dublin 4; tel: 283 7166; fax: 283 9419.* Open Mon–Sat 5–11pm, Sun

4–9.30pm. In the heart of Donnybrook village, where it's difficult to eat in a restaurant that's not rewarding, this one stands just a bit above the rest. The atmosphere is relaxed and candlelit. The food offers vegetarian choices but relies on seafood and pasta.

O'Connells in Ballsbridge €€€€ *Merrion Road, Ballsbridge, Dublin 4; tel: 647 3304; fax: 647 3398.* Open Mon–Sat 12.30–2.30pm, Sun 12.30–3pm; Mon–Sat 6–10.30pm, Sun 6–9.30pm. Located in the Bewley's Hotel on Merrion Road, the grounds date back to the 1880's but the food here is modern and utilises the very best in fresh Irish ingredients. Expect delicious roast and fresh seafood.

OUTSIDE DUBLIN

Cruzzo Bar & Restaurant €€€ *Marina Village, Malahide, County Dublin; tel: 845 0599; fax: 845 0602.* Open Tues–Fri 12.30–2.30pm, Sun 12.30–3.15pm; Tues–Fri and Sun 6–10pm, Sat 6–10.30pm. Situated in the picturesque Malahide marina, the bar and restaurant are built on a platform held high above the water on columns. Original paintings adorn the walls; fresh seafood (of course) fills the plates.

King Sitric €€€ *East Pier, Howth, County Dublin; tel: 832 5235.* Open Mon–Fri noon–2.15pm, Mon–Sat 6.30–11pm, closed Sun. Named after the first king of Dublin and housed in a Georgian residence, this restaurant has a good reputation for seafood. Rather pricey. Reservations recommended.

PD's Woodhouse €€ *2 Coliemore Road; tel: 284 9399.* Open daily 6–11pm. This well-known bistro is the place to enjoy excellent steaks and wild Irish salmon prepared on the unique oakwood barbecue grill.

Vermilion Indian Fusion Cuisine €€ *94–96 Terenure Road North, Dublin 6W; tel: 499 1400; fax: 499 1300; <www.vermilion.ie.>* Open daily 6pm–late, Sun from 1.30pm. The designers have fused hip European style with masala, with great success.

INDEX